CLEP
US History I Exam

SECRETS

Study Guide
Your Key to Exam Success

CLEP Test Review for the
College Level Examination Program

Dear Future Exam Success Story:

First of all, **THANK YOU** for purchasing Mometrix study materials!

Second, congratulations! You are one of the few determined test-takers who are committed to doing whatever it takes to excel on your exam. **You have come to the right place.** We developed these study materials with one goal in mind: to deliver you the information you need in a format that's concise and easy to use.

In addition to optimizing your guide for the content of the test, we've outlined our recommended steps for breaking down the preparation process into small, attainable goals so you can make sure you stay on track.

We've also analyzed the entire test-taking process, identifying the most common pitfalls and showing how you can overcome them and be ready for any curveball the test throws you.

Standardized testing is one of the biggest obstacles on your road to success, which only increases the importance of doing well in the high-pressure, high-stakes environment of test day. Your results on this test could have a significant impact on your future, and this guide provides the information and practical advice to help you achieve your full potential on test day.

Your success is our success

We would love to hear from you! If you would like to share the story of your exam success or if you have any questions or comments in regard to our products, please contact us at **800-673-8175** or **support@mometrix.com**.

Thanks again for your business and we wish you continued success!

Sincerely,
The Mometrix Test Preparation Team

Need more help? Check out our flashcards at: <u>http://MometrixFlashcards.com/CLEP</u>

TABLE OF CONTENTS

Introduction

Thank you for purchasing this resource! You have made the choice to prepare yourself for a test that could have a huge impact on your future, and this guide is designed to help you be fully ready for test day. Obviously, it's important to have a solid understanding of the test material, but you also need to be prepared for the unique environment and stressors of the test, so that you can perform to the best of your abilities.

For this purpose, the first section that appears in this guide is the **Secret Keys**. We've devoted countless hours to meticulously researching what works and what doesn't, and we've boiled down our findings to the five most impactful steps you can take to improve your performance on the test. We start at the beginning with study planning and move through the preparation process, all the way to the testing strategies that will help you get the most out of what you know when you're finally sitting in front of the test.

We recommend that you start preparing for your test as far in advance as possible. However, if you've bought this guide as a last-minute study resource and only have a few days before your test, we recommend that you skip over the first two Secret Keys since they address a long-term study plan.

If you struggle with **test anxiety**, we strongly encourage you to check out our recommendations for how you can overcome it. Test anxiety is a formidable foe, but it can be beaten, and we want to make sure you have the tools you need to defeat it.

Secret Key #1 – Plan Big, Study Small

There's a lot riding on your performance. If you want to ace this test, you're going to need to keep your skills sharp and the material fresh in your mind. You need a plan that lets you review everything you need to know while still fitting in your schedule. We'll break this strategy down into three categories.

Information Organization

Start with the information you already have: the official test outline. From this, you can make a complete list of all the concepts you need to cover before the test. Organize these concepts into groups that can be studied together, and create a list of any related vocabulary you need to learn so you can brush up on any difficult terms. You'll want to keep this vocabulary list handy once you actually start studying since you may need to add to it along the way.

Time Management

Once you have your set of study concepts, decide how to spread them out over the time you have left before the test. Break your study plan into small, clear goals so you have a manageable task for each day and know exactly what you're doing. Then just focus on one small step at a time. When you manage your time this way, you don't need to spend hours at a time studying. Studying a small block of content for a short period each day helps you retain information better and avoid stressing over how much you have left to do. You can relax knowing that you have a plan to cover everything in time. In order for this strategy to be effective though, you have to start studying early and stick to your schedule. Avoid the exhaustion and futility that comes from last-minute cramming!

Study Environment

The environment you study in has a big impact on your learning. Studying in a coffee shop, while probably more enjoyable, is not likely to be as fruitful as studying in a quiet room. It's important to keep distractions to a minimum. You're only planning to study for a short block of time, so make the most of it. Don't pause to check your phone or get up to find a snack. It's also important to **avoid multitasking**. Research has consistently shown that multitasking will make your studying dramatically less effective. Your study area should also be comfortable and well-lit so you don't have the distraction of straining your eyes or sitting on an uncomfortable chair.

The time of day you study is also important. You want to be rested and alert. Don't wait until just before bedtime. Study when you'll be most likely to comprehend and remember. Even better, if you know what time of day your test will be, set that time aside for study. That way your brain will be used to working on that subject at that specific time and you'll have a better chance of recalling information.

Finally, it can be helpful to team up with others who are studying for the same test. Your actual studying should be done in as isolated an environment as possible, but the work of organizing the information and setting up the study plan can be divided up. In between study sessions, you can discuss with your teammates the concepts that you're all studying and quiz each other on the details. Just be sure that your teammates are as serious about the test as you are. If you find that your study time is being replaced with social time, you might need to find a new team.

Secret Key #2 – Make Your Studying Count

You're devoting a lot of time and effort to preparing for this test, so you want to be absolutely certain it will pay off. This means doing more than just reading the content and hoping you can remember it on test day. It's important to make every minute of study count. There are two main areas you can focus on to make your studying count:

Retention

It doesn't matter how much time you study if you can't remember the material. You need to make sure you are retaining the concepts. To check your retention of the information you're learning, try recalling it at later times with minimal prompting. Try carrying around flashcards and glance at one or two from time to time or ask a friend who's also studying for the test to quiz you.

To enhance your retention, look for ways to put the information into practice so that you can apply it rather than simply recalling it. If you're using the information in practical ways, it will be much easier to remember. Similarly, it helps to solidify a concept in your mind if you're not only reading it to yourself but also explaining it to someone else. Ask a friend to let you teach them about a concept you're a little shaky on (or speak aloud to an imaginary audience if necessary). As you try to summarize, define, give examples, and answer your friend's questions, you'll understand the concepts better and they will stay with you longer. Finally, step back for a big picture view and ask yourself how each piece of information fits with the whole subject. When you link the different concepts together and see them working together as a whole, it's easier to remember the individual components.

Finally, practice showing your work on any multi-step problems, even if you're just studying. Writing out each step you take to solve a problem will help solidify the process in your mind, and you'll be more likely to remember it during the test.

Modality

Modality simply refers to the means or method by which you study. Choosing a study modality that fits your own individual learning style is crucial. No two people learn best in exactly the same way, so it's important to know your strengths and use them to your advantage.

For example, if you learn best by visualization, focus on visualizing a concept in your mind and draw an image or a diagram. Try color-coding your notes, illustrating them, or creating symbols that will trigger your mind to recall a learned concept. If you learn best by hearing or discussing information, find a study partner who learns the same way or read aloud to yourself. Think about how to put the information in your own words. Imagine that you are giving a lecture on the topic and record yourself so you can listen to it later.

For any learning style, flashcards can be helpful. Organize the information so you can take advantage of spare moments to review. Underline key words or phrases. Use different colors for different categories. Mnemonic devices (such as creating a short list in which every item starts with the same letter) can also help with retention. Find what works best for you and use it to store the information in your mind most effectively and easily.

Secret Key #3 – Practice the Right Way

Your success on test day depends not only on how many hours you put into preparing, but also on whether you prepared the right way. It's good to check along the way to see if your studying is paying off. One of the most effective ways to do this is by taking practice tests to evaluate your progress. Practice tests are useful because they show exactly where you need to improve. Every time you take a practice test, pay special attention to these three groups of questions:

- The questions you got wrong
- The questions you had to guess on, even if you guessed right
- The questions you found difficult or slow to work through

This will show you exactly what your weak areas are, and where you need to devote more study time. Ask yourself why each of these questions gave you trouble. Was it because you didn't understand the material? Was it because you didn't remember the vocabulary? Do you need more repetitions on this type of question to build speed and confidence? Dig into those questions and figure out how you can strengthen your weak areas as you go back to review the material.

Additionally, many practice tests have a section explaining the answer choices. It can be tempting to read the explanation and think that you now have a good understanding of the concept. However, an explanation likely only covers part of the question's broader context. Even if the explanation makes sense, **go back and investigate** every concept related to the question until you're positive you have a thorough understanding.

As you go along, keep in mind that the practice test is just that: practice. Memorizing these questions and answers will not be very helpful on the actual test because it is unlikely to have any of the same exact questions. If you only know the right answers to the sample questions, you won't be prepared for the real thing. **Study the concepts** until you understand them fully, and then you'll be able to answer any question that shows up on the test.

It's important to wait on the practice tests until you're ready. If you take a test on your first day of study, you may be overwhelmed by the amount of material covered and how much you need to learn. Work up to it gradually.

On test day, you'll need to be prepared for answering questions, managing your time, and using the test-taking strategies you've learned. It's a lot to balance, like a mental marathon that will have a big impact on your future. Like training for a marathon, you'll need to start slowly and work your way up. When test day arrives, you'll be ready.

Start with the strategies you've read in the first two Secret Keys—plan your course and study in the way that works best for you. If you have time, consider using multiple study resources to get different approaches to the same concepts. It can be helpful to see difficult concepts from more than one angle. Then find a good source for practice tests. Many times, the test website will suggest potential study resources or provide sample tests.

Practice Test Strategy

When you're ready to start taking practice tests, follow this strategy:

Untimed and Open-Book Practice

Take the first test with no time constraints and with your notes and study guide handy. Take your time and focus on applying the strategies you've learned.

Timed and Open-Book Practice

Take the second practice test open-book as well, but set a timer and practice pacing yourself to finish in time.

Timed and Closed-Book Practice

Take any other practice tests as if it were test day. Set a timer and put away your study materials. Sit at a table or desk in a quiet room, imagine yourself at the testing center, and answer questions as quickly and accurately as possible.

Keep repeating timed and closed-book tests on a regular basis until you run out of practice tests or it's time for the actual test. Your mind will be ready for the schedule and stress of test day, and you'll be able to focus on recalling the material you've learned.

Secret Key #4 – Pace Yourself

Once you're fully prepared for the material on the test, your biggest challenge on test day will be managing your time. Just knowing that the clock is ticking can make you panic even if you have plenty of time left. Work on pacing yourself so you can build confidence against the time constraints of the exam. Pacing is a difficult skill to master, especially in a high-pressure environment, so **practice is vital**.

Set time expectations for your pace based on how much time is available. For example, if a section has 60 questions and the time limit is 30 minutes, you know you have to average 30 seconds or less per question in order to answer them all. Although 30 seconds is the hard limit, set 25 seconds per question as your goal, so you reserve extra time to spend on harder questions. When you budget extra time for the harder questions, you no longer have any reason to stress when those questions take longer to answer.

Don't let this time expectation distract you from working through the test at a calm, steady pace, but keep it in mind so you don't spend too much time on any one question. Recognize that taking extra time on one question you don't understand may keep you from answering two that you do understand later in the test. If your time limit for a question is up and you're still not sure of the answer, mark it and move on, and come back to it later if the time and the test format allow. If the testing format doesn't allow you to return to earlier questions, just make an educated guess; then put it out of your mind and move on.

On the easier questions, be careful not to rush. It may seem wise to hurry through them so you have more time for the challenging ones, but it's not worth missing one if you know the concept and just didn't take the time to read the question fully. Work efficiently but make sure you understand the question and have looked at all of the answer choices, since more than one may seem right at first.

Even if you're paying attention to the time, you may find yourself a little behind at some point. You should speed up to get back on track, but do so wisely. Don't panic; just take a few seconds less on each question until you're caught up. Don't guess without thinking, but do look through the answer choices and eliminate any you know are wrong. If you can get down to two choices, it is often worthwhile to guess from those. Once you've chosen an answer, move on and don't dwell on any that you skipped or had to hurry through. If a question was taking too long, chances are it was one of the harder ones, so you weren't as likely to get it right anyway.

On the other hand, if you find yourself getting ahead of schedule, it may be beneficial to slow down a little. The more quickly you work, the more likely you are to make a careless mistake that will affect your score. You've budgeted time for each question, so don't be afraid to spend that time. Practice an efficient but careful pace to get the most out of the time you have.

Secret Key #5 – Have a Plan for Guessing

When you're taking the test, you may find yourself stuck on a question. Some of the answer choices seem better than others, but you don't see the one answer choice that is obviously correct. What do you do?

The scenario described above is very common, yet most test takers have not effectively prepared for it. Developing and practicing a plan for guessing may be one of the single most effective uses of your time as you get ready for the exam.

In developing your plan for guessing, there are three questions to address:

- When should you start the guessing process?
- How should you narrow down the choices?
- Which answer should you choose?

When to Start the Guessing Process

Unless your plan for guessing is to select C every time (which, despite its merits, is not what we recommend), you need to leave yourself enough time to apply your answer elimination strategies. Since you have a limited amount of time for each question, that means that if you're going to give yourself the best shot at guessing correctly, you have to decide quickly whether or not you will guess.

Of course, the best-case scenario is that you don't have to guess at all, so first, see if you can answer the question based on your knowledge of the subject and basic reasoning skills. Focus on the key words in the question and try to jog your memory of related topics. Give yourself a chance to bring the knowledge to mind, but once you realize that you don't have (or you can't access) the knowledge you need to answer the question, it's time to start the guessing process.

It's almost always better to start the guessing process too early than too late. It only takes a few seconds to remember something and answer the question from knowledge. Carefully eliminating wrong answer choices takes longer. Plus, going through the process of eliminating answer choices can actually help jog your memory.

Summary: Start the guessing process as soon as you decide that you can't answer the question based on your knowledge.

How to Narrow Down the Choices

The next chapter in this book (**Test-Taking Strategies**) includes a wide range of strategies for how to approach questions and how to look for answer choices to eliminate. You will definitely want to read those carefully, practice them, and figure out which ones work best for you. Here though, we're going to address a mindset rather than a particular strategy.

Your chances of guessing an answer correctly depend on how many options you are choosing from.

How many choices you have	How likely you are to guess correctly
5	20%
4	25%
3	33%
2	50%
1	100%

You can see from this chart just how valuable it is to be able to eliminate incorrect answers and make an educated guess, but there are two things that many test takers do that cause them to miss out on the benefits of guessing:

- Accidentally eliminating the correct answer
- Selecting an answer based on an impression

We'll look at the first one here, and the second one in the next section.

To avoid accidentally eliminating the correct answer, we recommend a thought exercise called **the $5 challenge**. In this challenge, you only eliminate an answer choice from contention if you are willing to bet $5 on it being wrong. Why $5? Five dollars is a small but not insignificant amount of money. It's an amount you could afford to lose but wouldn't want to throw away. And while losing $5 once might not hurt too much, doing it twenty times will set you back $100. In the same way, each small decision you make—eliminating a choice here, guessing on a question there—won't by itself impact your score very much, but when you put them all together, they can make a big difference. By holding each answer choice elimination decision to a higher standard, you can reduce the risk of accidentally eliminating the correct answer.

The $5 challenge can also be applied in a positive sense: If you are willing to bet $5 that an answer choice *is* correct, go ahead and mark it as correct.

Summary: Only eliminate an answer choice if you are willing to bet $5 that it is wrong.

Which Answer to Choose

You're taking the test. You've run into a hard question and decided you'll have to guess. You've eliminated all the answer choices you're willing to bet $5 on. Now you have to pick an answer. Why do we even need to talk about this? Why can't you just pick whichever one you feel like when the time comes?

The answer to these questions is that if you don't come into the test with a plan, you'll rely on your impression to select an answer choice, and if you do that, you risk falling into a trap. The test writers know that everyone who takes their test will be guessing on some of the questions, so they intentionally write wrong answer choices to seem plausible. You still have to pick an answer though, and if the wrong answer choices are designed to look right, how can you ever be sure that you're not falling for their trap? The best solution we've found to this dilemma is to take the decision out of your hands entirely. Here is the process we recommend:

Once you've eliminated any choices that you are confident (willing to bet $5) are wrong, select the first remaining choice as your answer.

Whether you choose to select the first remaining choice, the second, or the last, the important thing is that you use some preselected standard. Using this approach guarantees that you will not be enticed into selecting an answer choice that looks right, because you are not basing your decision on how the answer choices look.

This is not meant to make you question your knowledge. Instead, it is to help you recognize the difference between your knowledge and your impressions. There's a huge difference between thinking an answer is right because of what you know, and thinking an answer is right because it looks or sounds like it should be right.

Summary: To ensure that your selection is appropriately random, make a predetermined selection from among all answer choices you have not eliminated.

Test-Taking Strategies

This section contains a list of test-taking strategies that you may find helpful as you work through the test. By taking what you know and applying logical thought, you can maximize your chances of answering any question correctly!

It is very important to realize that every question is different and every person is different: no single strategy will work on every question, and no single strategy will work for every person. That's why we've included all of them here, so you can try them out and determine which ones work best for different types of questions and which ones work best for you.

Question Strategies

Read Carefully

Read the question and answer choices carefully. Don't miss the question because you misread the terms. You have plenty of time to read each question thoroughly and make sure you understand what is being asked. Yet a happy medium must be attained, so don't waste too much time. You must read carefully, but efficiently.

Contextual Clues

Look for contextual clues. If the question includes a word you are not familiar with, look at the immediate context for some indication of what the word might mean. Contextual clues can often give you all the information you need to decipher the meaning of an unfamiliar word. Even if you can't determine the meaning, you may be able to narrow down the possibilities enough to make a solid guess at the answer to the question.

Prefixes

If you're having trouble with a word in the question or answer choices, try dissecting it. Take advantage of every clue that the word might include. Prefixes and suffixes can be a huge help. Usually they allow you to determine a basic meaning. Pre- means before, post- means after, pro - is positive, de- is negative. From prefixes and suffixes, you can get an idea of the general meaning of the word and try to put it into context.

Hedge Words

Watch out for critical hedge words, such as *likely, may, can, sometimes, often, almost, mostly, usually, generally, rarely,* and *sometimes.* Question writers insert these hedge phrases to cover every possibility. Often an answer choice will be wrong simply because it leaves no room for exception. Be on guard for answer choices that have definitive words such as *exactly* and *always.*

Switchback Words

Stay alert for *switchbacks.* These are the words and phrases frequently used to alert you to shifts in thought. The most common switchback words are *but, although,* and *however.* Others include *nevertheless, on the other hand, even though, while, in spite of, despite, regardless of.* Switchback words are important to catch because they can change the direction of the question or an answer choice.

Face Value

When in doubt, use common sense. Accept the situation in the problem at face value. Don't read too much into it. These problems will not require you to make wild assumptions. If you have to go beyond creativity and warp time or space in order to have an answer choice fit the question, then you should move on and consider the other answer choices. These are normal problems rooted in reality. The applicable relationship or explanation may not be readily apparent, but it is there for you to figure out. Use your common sense to interpret anything that isn't clear.

Answer Choice Strategies

Answer Selection

The most thorough way to pick an answer choice is to identify and eliminate wrong answers until only one is left, then confirm it is the correct answer. Sometimes an answer choice may immediately seem right, but be careful. The test writers will usually put more than one reasonable answer choice on each question, so take a second to read all of them and make sure that the other choices are not equally obvious. As long as you have time left, it is better to read every answer choice than to pick the first one that looks right without checking the others.

Answer Choice Families

An answer choice family consists of two (in rare cases, three) answer choices that are very similar in construction and cannot all be true at the same time. If you see two answer choices that are direct opposites or parallels, one of them is usually the correct answer. For instance, if one answer choice says that quantity x increases and another either says that quantity x decreases (opposite) or says that quantity y increases (parallel), then those answer choices would fall into the same family. An answer choice that doesn't match the construction of the answer choice family is more likely to be incorrect. Most questions will not have answer choice families, but when they do appear, you should be prepared to recognize them.

Eliminate Answers

Eliminate answer choices as soon as you realize they are wrong, but make sure you consider all possibilities. If you are eliminating answer choices and realize that the last one you are left with is also wrong, don't panic. Start over and consider each choice again. There may be something you missed the first time that you will realize on the second pass.

Avoid Fact Traps

Don't be distracted by an answer choice that is factually true but doesn't answer the question. You are looking for the choice that answers the question. Stay focused on what the question is asking for so you don't accidentally pick an answer that is true but incorrect. Always go back to the question and make sure the answer choice you've selected actually answers the question and is not merely a true statement.

Extreme Statements

In general, you should avoid answers that put forth extreme actions as standard practice or proclaim controversial ideas as established fact. An answer choice that states the "process should be used in certain situations, if..." is much more likely to be correct than one that states the "process should be discontinued completely." The first is a calm rational statement and doesn't even make a definitive, uncompromising stance, using a hedge word *if* to provide wiggle room, whereas the second choice is a radical idea and far more extreme.

Benchmark

As you read through the answer choices and you come across one that seems to answer the question well, mentally select that answer choice. This is not your final answer, but it's the one that will help you evaluate the other answer choices. The one that you selected is your benchmark or standard for judging each of the other answer choices. Every other answer choice must be compared to your benchmark. That choice is correct until proven otherwise by another answer choice beating it. If you find a better answer, then that one becomes your new benchmark. Once you've decided that no other choice answers the question as well as your benchmark, you have your final answer.

Predict the Answer

Before you even start looking at the answer choices, it is often best to try to predict the answer. When you come up with the answer on your own, it is easier to avoid distractions and traps because you will know exactly what to look for. The right answer choice is unlikely to be word-for-word what you came up with, but it should be a close match. Even if you are confident that you have the right answer, you should still take the time to read each option before moving on.

General Strategies

Tough Questions

If you are stumped on a problem or it appears too hard or too difficult, don't waste time. Move on! Remember though, if you can quickly check for obviously incorrect answer choices, your chances of guessing correctly are greatly improved. Before you completely give up, at least try to knock out a couple of possible answers. Eliminate what you can and then guess at the remaining answer choices before moving on.

Check Your Work

Since you will probably not know every term listed and the answer to every question, it is important that you get credit for the ones that you do know. Don't miss any questions through careless mistakes. If at all possible, try to take a second to look back over your answer selection and make sure you've selected the correct answer choice and haven't made a costly careless mistake (such as marking an answer choice that you didn't mean to mark). This quick double check should more than pay for itself in caught mistakes for the time it costs.

Pace Yourself

It's easy to be overwhelmed when you're looking at a page full of questions; your mind is confused and full of random thoughts, and the clock is ticking down faster than you would like. Calm down and maintain the pace that you have set for yourself. Especially as you get down to the last few minutes of the test, don't let the small numbers on the clock make you panic. As long as you are on track by monitoring your pace, you are guaranteed to have time for each question.

Don't Rush

It is very easy to make errors when you are in a hurry. Maintaining a fast pace in answering questions is pointless if it makes you miss questions that you would have gotten right otherwise. Test writers like to include distracting information and wrong answers that seem right. Taking a little extra time to avoid careless mistakes can make all the difference in your test score. Find a pace that allows you to be confident in the answers that you select.

Keep Moving

Panicking will not help you pass the test, so do your best to stay calm and keep moving. Taking deep breaths and going through the answer elimination steps you practiced can help to break through a stress barrier and keep your pace.

Final Notes

The combination of a solid foundation of content knowledge and the confidence that comes from practicing your plan for applying that knowledge is the key to maximizing your performance on test day. As your foundation of content knowledge is built up and strengthened, you'll find that the strategies included in this chapter become more and more effective in helping you quickly sift through the distractions and traps of the test to isolate the correct answer.

Now it's time to move on to the test content chapters of this book, but be sure to keep your goal in mind. As you read, think about how you will be able to apply this information on the test. If you've already seen sample questions for the test and you have an idea of the question format and style, try to come up with questions of your own that you can answer based on what you're reading. This will give you valuable practice applying your knowledge in the same ways you can expect to on test day.

Good luck and good studying!

History of the United States: 1500 to 1789

Ch 3

First European Explorers in America

Although **Christopher Columbus** frequently gets credit for "discovering" America (notwithstanding the fact that people were already living on the continent), **Vikings** from Scandinavia actually arrived in about A.D. 1000. These explorers constructed no permanent settlements, however, and did not remain for long. It was not until economic expansion in Europe made exploration worthwhile that explorers would return. Columbus, and the explorers who would come later, were looking for the **Northwest Passage** that would take them directly to Asia and were actually annoyed by the new land that kept getting in the way. Columbus actually died believing that he had landed in some outpost of India (hence, "Indians").

> **Review Video: Christopher Columbus**
> Visit mometrix.com/academy and enter code: 496598

English Interest in the New World

The English lagged somewhat behind other European nations in exploration of the New World. Finally, however, a combination of economic and social incentives convinced them to look west. For one thing, the **enclosure movement** in England had made land very scarce, and the practice of **primogeniture** meant that only the eldest son could inherit the land. For these reasons, many Englishmen moved to the New World for the promise of cheap land. England also had a large population at this time and thus the government viewed the New World as a good place to send criminals and beggars. Another reason for the increase in interest in America was the **Protestant Reformation**. Many English Catholics and Protestants felt alienated by the new Church of England, and wanted to find somewhere in which they could worship more freely.

> **Review Video: The Reformation: Martin Luther**
> Visit mometrix.com/academy and enter code: 691828

Settling of North America by the English

The first English attempt to found a colony in the New World was made by Sir Humphrey Gilbert in **Newfoundland** in 1583, and was a complete failure. Sir Walter Raleigh would lead two more failed attempts at founding a colony on **Roanoke Island** in 1586 and 1588. The second of these colonies is known as the **Lost Colony**, because it disappeared without a trace while Raleigh was gone. Finally, the British were able to establish a permanent colony at **Jamestown**, Virginia in 1607. The settlers in Jamestown came for gold and to convert the Natives to Christianity. One of the important events of the early years of Jamestown was the issuing of the Virginia Charter, which declared that English settlers in the New World would be treated as Englishmen with full English rights.

> **Review Video: Jamestown**
> Visit mometrix.com/academy and enter code: 881040

Virginia Colony

Beginnings

The English colony of **Virginia**, which began at Jamestown, was at first plagued by a poor location and a paucity of skilled laborers. Captain **John Smith** was elected leader in 1608, and he proved to

- 15 -

be the strict leader the colony needed to survive. A large proportion of the settlers would die during the winter of 1609-10. What finally saved the Virginia colony was the wild popularity of **tobacco**. In 1619, the **House of Burgesses** met, becoming the first legislative body to be formed in the New World. King James I of England correctly predicted that this would only lead to trouble for his nation. Also in 1619, 20 African indentured servants arrived on a Dutch warship; Virginia would become the first colony to legalize **slavery**, in 1660.

> **Review Video: The English Colony of Virginia**
> Visit mometrix.com/academy and enter code: 537399

Royal Colony

Virginia officially became a **Royal Colony** in 1624. This was in part because the Virginia Company (the joint-stock company that had previously administered affairs) had gone bankrupt, and partly because King James I wanted to exercise more control. After the English Civil War of the 1640s, many of the supporters of the king, known as **cavaliers**, settled in Virginia. During this period, the wealthy colonists began claiming the coastal land and pushing the poor people farther inland, where they were prey to Indian attacks and were underrepresented in the House of Burgesses. Frustrated, a group of settlers led by **Nathaniel Bacon** burned Jamestown to the ground. **Bacon's Rebellion**, as it came to be known, is thought of by some as a harbinger of things to come.

Beginnings of English Colonies of Maryland, the Carolinas, and Georgia

Maryland was established in 1634 as a **proprietary colony**, meaning it was exclusively owned by one person. The owner, Lord Baltimore, ran his colony like a feudal estate. Maryland prospered because of tobacco and became a haven for persecuted Catholics. **North Carolina** was originally settled by Virginians, and quickly acquired a reputation as independent and democratic. Many English colonists avoided North Carolina because they felt it was overrun by pirates. **South Carolina**, meanwhile, was a proprietary colony established in 1670. South Carolina hosted a large number of religious groups. **Georgia**, meanwhile, was a proprietary colony established in 1733. Its namesake, George II, hoped that it would be a buffer zone between the colonists and the Indians, and populated it almost exclusively with criminals and debtors.

Southern Colonies

Economic Life

In the early days of the Southern colonies, most people lived on **small farms**. Although they made up a tiny part of the population, the owners of the **coastal plantations** wielded enormous power. These aristocrats typically grew a single crop on their lands: in North Carolina, Virginia, and Maryland, **tobacco** was the cash crop, while the large growers in South Carolina and Georgia favored **rice** and **indigo**. Plantations, like the feudal manors of the past, were almost totally self-sufficient units, although the owners imported most of their luxury items from England. The Southern colonies had the closest ties with England, mainly because England provided the market for their tobacco; crops grown in the colonies were sold back in England by agents (known as factors).

Social Life

The social lives of the Southern colonists were filled with dancing, card-playing, cotillions, hunts, and large community dinners. Southerners were considered to be very optimistic in temperament, in contrast to their more dour Northern counterparts. It was extremely difficult to move up in the **social hierarchy** in the South; the richer colonists generally took the best land and thus were able to maintain their position in the economy and in the government, as the poor had to move away from the towns to find farmland. Because farming was the only available occupation, there were not any venues for ambitious men to distinguish themselves. North Carolina was generally considered to be the state with the least **social stratification**.

Life Expectancy and Education

The average man in the Southern colonies could expect to live **35 years**. This was in part due to disease; stagnant water and unfamiliar heat helped the spread of many contagions throughout the population, and malaria was a constant danger. Because of the high mortality rate, most families were very large. Also, **education** was not a high priority in the colonies in those days. One problem was that the population was too scattered for a central public school to be possible. Wealthy plantation owners would hire a **tutor** for their children, who might later be sent off to William and Mary or one of the new schools up North: Harvard, Yale, or Princeton. For the less affluent, however, it was more likely that any education would be received as an **apprentice** of an experienced craftsman.

Religious and Political Life

In all of the Southern colonies, the **Anglican Church** was supported by taxes. Anyone who wanted to enter politics would have to be a member of the Church, though the majority of the colonists were not. In general, the Southern colonies had the greatest degree of **religious toleration**. Politics during this period were largely controlled by the planter aristocracy. Each Southern colony had a **governor** (chosen by the colony's English sponsor), a **governor's council**, and an **assembly** to represent the people. During the 1700s, these assemblies took more and more power away from the governors. In order to run for office, a man had to be a member of the Anglican Church; many people, including Thomas Jefferson, would acquire membership in the Church and then never set foot inside it again.

h4

Beginning of Slave Trade

After periods in which Native Americans or indentured servants from England were used as laborers, most of the labor in the Southern British North American colonies was performed by **African slaves**. These slaves were taken in wars between African chieftains, and then sold to European traders. Oftentimes, the African leaders would trade slaves for guns in order to protect themselves from other slave traders. Several African states, most notably the Yoruba and the Dahomey, became wealthy from this trade. The journey from West Africa to the West Indies was dangerous and depressing, and many slaves died en route. Before they were sold into the American colonies, slaves first worked in the brutal heat of the sugar plantations of the British West Indies. Only about half would survive long enough to see America.

Legalization of Slavery

Between 1640 and 1660, the Southern colonies slowly evolved from a system of servitude to one of **slavery**. In 1661, Virginia became the first colony to legalize **chattel slavery for life**, and made it such that the children of slaves would be slaves as well. The number of slaves increased dramatically in the 1680s after the **Royal African Company** lost its monopoly and the industry was thrown open to anyone. Virginia established **slave codes** to keep revolts down: slaves could not be taught to read, could not gather together, could not have weapons, and could not leave the plantation without written permission. Naturally, slaves often rebelled against their treatment, but they were outnumbered and overpowered.

> **Review Video: Southern Colonies: An Overview**
> Visit mometrix.com/academy and enter code: 703830
>
> **Review Video: Southern Colonies: Family Life and Education**
> Visit mometrix.com/academy and enter code: 881049
>
> **Review Video: Southern Colonies: Religion and Politics**
> Visit mometrix.com/academy and enter code: 515423
>
> **Review Video: Plantation System**
> Visit mometrix.com/academy and enter code: 272285

Early Resistance to Slavery

Many slaves resisted submission, and many died as a result. For any serious offense, a slave would be executed in front of his or her peers as a deterrent. From its inception, there was **resistance** to slavery. In 1688, the **Quakers** declared that slavery was inhuman and a violation of the Bible. Many felt that slavery degraded both master and slave. In order to justify the hateful institution, slave-owners declared that blacks were less than human, or that, as descendants of the Biblical figure Ham, they were ordered by God to serve whites. The hymn "Amazing Grace" was written by guilt-wracked former slave trader **John Newton**. Slaves could only become free by proving mulatto (half white) status, or by buying their freedom (some masters would allow their slaves to work for pay on the weekends).

Puritanism and the Pilgrims in Massachusetts Colony

Puritans believe in the idea of predestination, meaning that God has already chosen which people will get into heaven. In order to suggest to others (and to themselves) that they were among the elect, **Puritans** were obsessed with maintaining proper decorum in public. Those Puritans who wanted to fully separate from the Church of England were known as **Pilgrims** (or Separatists). The Pilgrims originally went to Holland, but after determining that they would be unable to make a good life there, they got permission from the Virginia Company to settle in the northern part of the Virginia colony in 1620. The **Plymouth Company** was commissioned, and the **Mayflower** set sail. Because of storms and poor navigation, however, they ended up in the area that would come to be known as Massachusetts. One of the early moves of the group was to agree to the **Mayflower Compact**, whereby all members of the group would be bound to the will of the majority.

> **Review Video: The Mayflower Compact**
> Visit mometrix.com/academy and enter code: 275859

Puritans

The Puritans established the colony of **Massachusetts Bay** in 1630. They hoped to purify the **Church of England** and then return to Europe with a new and improved religion. The Massachusetts Bay Puritans were more immediately successful than other fledgling colonies because they brought enough supplies, arrived in the springtime, and had good leadership (including **John Winthrop**). Puritans fished, cut timber for ships, and trapped fur. The local government was inextricably bound with the church; only church members were allowed to vote for the **General Court** (similar to the House of Burgesses), although everyone was required to pay taxes. The Puritans established a **Bible Commonwealth** that would last 50 years. During this time, Old Testament law was the law of the community.

Political and Social Life in the Early Massachusetts Colonies

The **Massachusetts Bay Puritans** were known for religious intolerance and a general suspicion of democracy. Even though they had left England because of religious persecution, they did not set up their colony as a safe haven for others. One of the people who was kicked out of the colony for blasphemy was **Roger Williams**, who went on to found a colony at **Providence**. Williams taught that the colonists should be fair to the Indians, and that political leaders should stay out of religion. Roger Williams eventually founded the **Baptist Church**. The Puritans generally felt that the common people were incapable of governing themselves and should be looked after by their government. Also, many Puritans objected to democracy because they felt it was inefficient.

English Civil War and the New England Confederation

During the English Civil War, the Puritans tried to separate from the Church of England; they issued the **Body of Liberties**, which stated that the Massachusetts Bay was independent of England and was therefore no longer bound by English Civil Law, that there could be no arbitrary governors appointed to dissolve a local legislature, and that town meetings of qualified voters would be held to discuss local issues. Later, in 1643, a **New England Confederation** was formed, consisting of Massachusetts Bay, New Plymouth, Connecticut River Valley, and New Haven. The goals of this confederation were to protect the colonists from the French (in Canada) and the Indians; to safeguard their commercial interests from the Dutch in New Netherlands (later New York); and to return runaway slaves.

Dominion of New England

The impertinence of the **Massachusetts Bay colony** was a constant annoyance to **King Charles II** and he thus punished them by granting charters to rival colonies in Connecticut and Rhode Island and by creating the **Dominion of New England**. The purpose of this organization was to boost trade by enforcing the **Navigation Acts** of 1660 and 1663, which stated that all trade had to be done on English ships and had to pass through England before it could go anywhere else. The English, of course, made the colonists pay a tax on any exports that were not bound for England. The colonists loathed the Dominion government, not only because of its economic penalties, but because it tried to promote the Anglican Church in America. A rebellion against the Dominion probably would have occurred if the **Glorious Revolution** in England had not ended it prematurely.

Review Video: Life in New England
Visit mometrix.com/academy and enter code: 551857

Land, Demography, Climate, Economics, and Slavery in Puritan life

The **land** settled by the Puritans was rocky and bare, and it took tremendous labor to subsist off of its products. Massachusetts had an extremely homogenous **population**, mainly because there was little reason to stay there other than to be among people of the same faith. Non-Puritan immigrants usually moved south, where the soil was better and the population was more tolerant. Because agriculture was so tricky, a more diverse **economy** developed in New England than existed in the South. Puritans engaged in fishing and trapping, and there were a number of craftsmen in each town. There were **slaves** in New England, though not nearly as many as in the South. Furthermore, slaves in New England were more commonly used as household servants than hard laborers.

Social and Religious Life of the Puritans

There was more chance for **social mobility** in Massachusetts than in any other colony in America. This was mainly due to the diverse economy. As for religion, it dominated every area of an individual's life. The Puritan Church was known as the **Congregational Church**; at first, this was an exclusive group, but it gradually became easier to become a member. Indeed, by the mid-1600s religious fervor seemed to be waning in Massachusetts. A group called the **Jeremiads** warned the people that they were in danger of lapsing into atheism, but many people did not mind. Around this time, ministers began to offer **half-way covenants**, which gave church members partial privileges.

Salem Witch Trials

During the 1690s in New England, there was still a strong belief in **Christian mysticism**. Many people were paranoid about spiritualists and mediums. This, combined with perhaps some local feuds, led to 19 women and one man being executed for **witchcraft** in 1692. Most likely, however, the accused individuals were only suffering from delusions caused by a kind of hallucinogenic bread mold (ergot). The witch trials only stopped when people in high places began being accused. The **Salem witch trials** tarnished the image of the clergy for a long time, and further contributed to a general relaxation of religious fervor in this period.

The Great Awakening

The Great Awakening was a religious revival in New England in the 1730s and 40s. It began in response to the growing secularism and was aided by the recent migrations into the cities, where it was easier for large crowds to form. **Jonathan Edwards** was one of the most famous preachers of this time. The **Great Awakening** was the first mass movement in America; it helped break down the divides between the various regions of the British colonies and led to the formation of some new Protestant denominations. Though the Revivalists did not directly advocate the abolition of slavery, they did suggest that there was divinity in all creation, and that therefore blacks were worthy of being converted to Christianity.

Review Video: The Great Awakening
Visit mometrix.com/academy and enter code: 327656

Bible Commonwealth and Political and Intellectual Life in New England

The New England colonies started out as **Bible Commonwealths**, where Biblical law was local law, and a man's standing in the church determined his political power. Over time, however, New England became more liberal, and politics came to be dominated by the **wealthy men** rather than by the church leaders. Life expectancy in the New England colonies became roughly what it is today. **Education** was valued greatly in New England, and the fact that most people lived close to a town made it possible for more people to receive an inexpensive training. Puritans believed that ignorance of God's word could lead one to be tricked by the devil, and thus they made sure that all of their children learned to read.

New Netherlands Colony

The Dutch East India Company hired the English explorer **Henry Hudson** to search for the Northwest Passage to Asia. Instead, he journeyed up the Hudson River and claimed the area now known as **New York** for the Dutch. The Dutch purchased **Manhattan Island** from the Manhattan Indians for $24, and established a town called **New Amsterdam** there, an aristocratic town, in which everyone had to be a member of the Dutch Reform Church. Eventually, in 1664, this Dutch settlement would be overwhelmed by the British colonies surrounding it. King Charles II gave the area to his successor, James, Duke of York, who quickly gave the town and colony the name it bears today.

Pennsylvania Colony, Quakers, and The Charter of Liberties

The Pennsylvania (literally "Penn's woods") colony was established by **William Penn** in 1681. Penn declared that the colony would provide religious and political freedom for all. The main religious group to settle in the area was the **Society of Friends** (Quakers). Quakers believed that every person could communicate with the divine, that the church should not be supported by tax dollars, and that all men are equal. The Quakers have always been pacifists, and they were the first group to oppose slavery. In Pennsylvania, voting rights were extended only to land holders or large taxpayers. The **Charter of Liberties** (1701) established a unicameral legislature working alongside a governor.

Middle Colonies

Economic Life, Slavery, and Society

The **Middle Colonies** (New York, Pennsylvania, Delaware, East and West New Jersey) shared characteristics with both New England and the Southern colonies. The **economy** was diverse, though less so than in New England. Shipping and commerce would gradually become crucial in the port cities of Philadelphia and New York. There were plenty of **slaves** in the Middle Colonies, most of whom served as laborers on ships. The Dutch treated their slaves well; the English did not. People in these colonies tended to have a healthier lifestyle than their neighbors to the south, and therefore they tended to live longer. The diverse economy made **social mobility** possible, though large landowners were for the most part entrenched in positions of power.

Education, Religion, and Politics

Most education in the Middle Colonies was received as an **apprentice** to a successful craftsman. Often, local churches would maintain schools during the week. The two main religious organizations in this region were the **Anglican Church** and the **Dutch Reform Church**, often at each other's throat because they were competing for members and tax dollars. A typical government in the Middle Colonies had a **governor**, a governor's council, and a **representative**

assembly. Men were only allowed to vote if they owned property. The Middle Colonies had the most diverse population, mainly because they had available land and promised religious freedom (at least in Pennsylvania).

George Grenville and the Proclamation of 1763

Ch 5

George Grenville became the prime minister of Britain in 1763, and immediately abandoned the policy of "salutary neglect" that had been upheld by Walpole. On the contrary, he asserted that the American colonists should have to pay for British military protection, even though the Americans claimed not to need it. According to the **Proclamation of 1763**, all American colonists were to stay east of the Appalachian Mountains. This policy was ostensibly created in order to protect the colonists in the wake of **Chief Pontiac's Rebellion** in 1763, in which Indians attacked colonists and were subsequently slaughtered by the British. Many colonists, however, felt that the Proclamation was a transparent attempt to maintain British control of the fur trade.

Sugar (Revenue) Act, Currency Act, and the Quartering Act

The Sugar (Revenue) Act of 1764 established a duty on basically any products that were not British in origin: for instance molasses, indigo, and sugar. Unlike the Molasses Act, the **Sugar Act** was fully enforced. Most colonists resented this taxation, which they felt was used to fund the French and Indian War. The **Currency Act of 1764** forbade colonists from issuing paper money, and stated that all taxes paid to England must be paid in gold and silver rather than paper. This act eliminated the worthless Continental Dollar. The **Quartering Act of 1765** required colonists to provide bedding and food to the regiments of British soldiers in America. This regulation increased paranoia amongst the colonists, who began to wonder exactly why the British soldiers were there in the first place.

Stamp Act of 1765

The Stamp Act of 1765 was levied without the consent of the colonists. It specified that a stamp must be applied to all legal documents (there was considerable debate over the definition of this phrase) indicating that a tax had been paid for the defense of the colonies. This act was extremely unpopular, perhaps most because its presence was so visible; its implementation generated loud cries of "**taxation without representation**." The British responded by claiming that the colonists had "virtual representation" by members of Parliament. The colonists continued to claim that they needed direct and actual representation, although many feared that even if they were to get it, they would probably lose most votes anyway.

Stamp Act Congress, the Sons of Liberty, and the Declaratory Act

The colonists created the Stamp Act Congress in New York in order to peacefully resolve the conflicts created by the Stamp Act. This group established the **Non-importation Agreements**, which amounted to a boycott of English products. At the same time, the **Sons of Liberty** in Boston were running amok: vandalizing British goods, tarring and feathering stamp collectors, and erecting so-called "liberty poles," from which collectors would be hung by their pants. In 1766, the new British prime minister **Rockingham** repealed the Stamp Act because the boycotts were damaging the British economy. In part to punish the colonists for their insubordination, in 1766 the British Parliament issued the **Declaratory Act**, which asserted that they had the right to legislate on behalf of the colonists at any time.

Townshend Acts

The Townshend Acts, named after Charles "Champagne Charlie" Townshend, the prime minister of Britain from 1766-1772, placed an indirect tax on household items coming into the colonies, and tightened the custom duties. The Acts also called for stricter vice-admiralty courts and established the **Writs of Assistance**, which were essentially blank search warrants. The colonists' response to the Townshend Acts was twofold: a **pamphlet war** was waged by men like John Dickinson, James Otis, and Samuel Adams; and there were also more violent protests, as for instance the **Boston Massacre**, in which a mob in the Boston Commons was fired on by the British, perhaps accidentally. Colonists used the "Massacre" as a rallying cry, and the Townshend Acts were repealed (with the notable exception of the tax on tea).

Lord North, the Gaspee, the Committees of Correspondence, and John Wilkes

Lord North succeeded Townshend as British prime minister in 1772. In this year, the Sons of Liberty set fire to the **Gaspee**, a British revenue ship, off the coast of Rhode Island. The Sons of Liberty were driven to further violence by Massachusetts governor Tom Hutchinson's announcement that his salary would be paid by the British. The **Committees of Correspondence** were subsequently formed to organize the protest against the British, and to keep colonists informed on British matters. At around this time, the British MP **John Wilkes** became a folk hero in the colonies because of his impassioned speeches in defense of liberty. Although Wilkes never spoke directly on behalf of the colonists, he was jailed for his speeches.

Coercive (Intolerable) Acts

The Coercive Acts, known as the **Intolerable Acts** in America, were issued in response to the Boston Tea Party, and had several parts. The **Boston Port Act** closed the port down, supposedly until such time as the destroyed tea was paid for, although this never happened. The **Massachusetts Government Act** put the colony under martial law. A military governor, Thomas Gage, was placed in charge of the colony. The **Administration of Justice Act** required that all judges, soldiers, and tax agents be English, and that all crimes be tried in England. The **New Quartering Act** asserted that British soldiers were allowed to enter private homes and demand lodging. The **Quebec Act of 1774** declared that everything west of the Appalachians was Quebec; although this was basically done so that Britain could govern more effectively, it caused speculation among the colonists that the British were going to sell America to the French.

First Continental Congress

The First Continental Congress was held September 5, 1774, and was attended by a representative of every colony except Georgia. This Congress issued the **Suffolk Resolves**, stating that they would give Boston aid in the form of food and clothing, but would not take up arms on behalf of Boston. The **Continental Association**, an agreement not to buy or sell English goods, was formed. A conservative named Joseph Galloway advocated the creation of a **Council of All Colonies**, a legislative body which would share power with Parliament. The **Galloway Plan** was nixed by Massachusetts, however, because that colony refused to share power with any British authority. Massachusetts at this time was in a highly volatile state.

Thomas Gage and Paul Revere

Thomas Gage, the military governor of Massachusetts, was under increasing duress at the beginning of 1775 and asked the British government for either 20,000 more troops or a repeal of the Coercive Acts. Instead, Britain sent 2,000 troops, which **Gage** used to collect guns, gunpowder, and shot. On April 18 of 1775, the British troops sailed across Boston Harbor toward the large stockpile at Concord. **Paul Revere** then took his famous ride to warn the other colonists about the approach of the British. Although Revere was captured, his ride was finished by Samuel Prescott and William Dawes. On the way to Concord, in Lexington, shots were fired and 8 colonial militiamen were killed. The British then moved on to Concord, where the real fighting began.

Second Continental Congress

The Second Continental Congress was held May 10, 1775 in Philadelphia. **George Washington** became the commander of the Americans, mainly because it was felt that he would be able to bring the Southern colonies into the fold. This Congress also drew up the **Olive Branch petition**, a peace offering made to the King of England. The **Articles of Confederation** were drawn up here; their emphasis on states' rights proved to be a poor setup for organizing a comprehensive military strategy. This Congress created the **Committees of Safety**, a system for training community militias. This Congress created a bureaucracy for the purpose of organizing a navy and raising money. Finally, it was here that the colonists formally declared **independence**.

> **Review Video:** <u>The First and Second Continental Congress</u>
> Visit mometrix.com/academy and enter code: 835211

Reasons for Declaring Independence

At the time that the Declaration of Independence was issued, many colonists were opposed to complete separation from England. Many of them still considered themselves Englishmen and were afraid to be branded as traitors. They also realized that they were in uncharted waters: no revolt had ever been successful in winning independence. Finally, many colonists feared that even if they were successful in winning independence, the result would be chaos in America. The minds of many of these reluctant colonists were changed, however, by the **Battle of Bunker Hill**, which was won by the British. After this battle, King George II declared that the colonists were in a state of rebellion. Furthermore, the British labeled the members of the **Second Continental Congress** as traitors and ignored the **Olive Branch petition**. Confused colonists were further flamed by the British use of Hessian mercenary soldiers. The writings of **Thomas Paine** also converted many colonists to the revolutionary cause.

Declaration of Independence

The Declaration of Independence was proposed at the **Second Continental Congress** by Richard Henry Lee, and was composed by a committee of Franklin, Jefferson, John Adams, Robert Livingston, and Roger Sherman. The document has three parts: a **preamble** and reasons for separation; a **theory of government**; and a formal **declaration of war**. Jefferson attempted to have it include a condemnation of slavery, but was rebuffed. The Declaration had many aims: to enlist help from other British colonies; to create a cause for which to fight; to motivate reluctant colonists; to ensure that captured Americans would be treated as prisoners of war; and to establish an American theory of government. In fulfilling this last purpose, Jefferson borrowed heavily from Enlightenment thinkers like Montesquieu, Rousseau, and Locke, asserting famously that "all men are created equal."

Significance

The issuing of the Declaration of Independence had effects both on the Revolutionary War and on world history at large. As far as its immediate effects, it changed the war in America from a war for liberty to a war for independence, by rhetorically **emancipating** America from Britain. It also

- 24 -

opened a path for the **French Revolution** a few years later, one motivated by the principles expressed in the Declaration. Revolutions in South America, Africa, and Asia have also used the Declaration of Independence as inspiration. In the subsequent history of the United States, the document would be used by **abolitionists** as an argument against slavery, and by **suffragists** as an argument for the right of women to vote.

> **Review Video:** <u>Declaration of Independence</u>
> Visit mometrix.com/academy and enter code: 256838

Saratoga Campaign

The British military plan during the early stages of the Revolutionary War was known as the **Saratoga campaign** (or the German Plan). It called for a three-pronged attack aimed at capturing New York and thus separating the Northeast from the Southern colonies. This plan broke down because of the following reasons: One of the generals, Howe, was supposed to go up the Hudson River to Albany, but instead decided to go after Philadelphia. Another general, Burgoyne, was able to conquer Fort Ticonderoga, but then languished without supplies for months, and eventually had to surrender to colonial troops. The third general, St. Ledger, made considerable progress across New York from Lake Ontario, but lost steam after a series of small battles.

Battle of Saratoga

The colonial General Gates defeated the British General Burgoyne at the **Battle of Saratoga** in 1777. This defeat confirmed the failure of the British Saratoga Campaign. More importantly, perhaps, it convinced the French that the Americans could win the war. The French then signed the **Treaty of Alliance** in 1778, which supplied the Americans with money, men, and ships. This treaty was in part negotiated by Benjamin Franklin. The French were not necessarily motivated by a spirit of goodwill towards the Americans; they hoped to gain back the territory they had lost in the French and Indian War. Moreover, the French believed that by aiding the Americans in the Revolutionary War they could position themselves to colonize parts of North America as yet unclaimed.

Southern Campaign in the Revolutionary War

The British military campaign in the **Southern colonies** was planned by Sir Henry Clinton and implemented by General Cornwallis in the years 1778 to 1781. Cornwallis quickly took **Savannah** and **Charleston** and then moved into the interior of South Carolina. Here and in North Carolina a series of bloody battles (many of them against the great American general Nathaniel Greene) weakened Cornwallis and forced him to make a supply run to **Yorktown** on the Virginia coast. There, the British suffered a naval defeat at the hands of the French, and then were routed by Washington-led troops. During their retreat, the British naval forces were further weakened by a violent storm, and Cornwallis was forced to **surrender** on October 17, 1781.

Legacy of the Revolutionary War

After the conclusion of the Revolutionary War, neither the Proclamation of 1763 nor the Quebec Act applied, and thus colonists could **move west** across the Appalachians. A few British loyalists lost their land. After the war, many states moved to separate the church and state; in Virginia, for instance, Thomas Jefferson wrote the **Virginia Statute of Religious Freedom**, creating total separation in that state. States also revised the **Criminal Codes**, in an effort to make the punishment more closely fit the crime. Finally, whereas in 1750 most citizens did not question the institution of slavery, by 1780 many states began to examine this policy. Vermont was the first state to **abolish slavery**. Meanwhile, Southern states argued that the war would not have been won without slave labor.

Review Video: The Revolutionary War
Visit mometrix.com/academy and enter code: 935282

Articles of Confederation

Ch6 (handwritten)

The Articles of Confederation were largely ineffective because they gave too much power to the states and too little to a central government. Many historians now say that the best thing about the **Articles** were that they showed the authors of the Constitution what to avoid. Part of the Articles was the **Land Ordinance of 1785**, a plan created by Jefferson for dividing the Western land into organized townships. The sale of land in these territories helped generate money for the new government. The **Northwest Ordinance of 1787** divided the land above the Ohio River into five territories, which would soon become states. This ordinance would become the model for how all future states would be formed.

Foreign Affairs

Both the Americans and the British violated the terms of the **Treaty of Paris**, which had ended the Revolutionary War in 1783. The British, for instance, never fully abandoned their lucrative fur trade in the Ohio Valley. Americans, on the other hand, never paid back their pre-war debts. Meanwhile, the Spanish (who controlled Louisiana and Florida) openly challenged American borders in the South, at times encouraging Native Americans to make war on the fledgling nation. Americans sought the right of deposit on the Mississippi; that is, the right to load material from a boat to a dock. The Spanish were not quick to grant this right. Meanwhile, American ships were forced to pay tribute to the Barbary states in order to trade in the Mediterranean.

Debt, Passing Legislation, Law Enforcement, the Court System, and Inflation and Depreciation

After the Revolutionary War, the United States found itself in a massive and troubling **debt**. Meanwhile, Congress was having great difficulty passing any **legislation** because in order to be made into law, a bill had to receive 9 of 13 votes, and there were often fewer than 10 representatives present. The government had no **chief executive**, and thus law enforcement was left to the states. Another major problem was that the lack of a **central court system** made it hard to resolve disputes between citizens from different states, or between the states themselves. Congress did not have the power to **tax** the people directly, and could only request funds. Furthermore, although Congress could issue **currency**, it had no authority to keep the states from issuing currency of their own, so wild inflation and depreciation were common.

Competing Currencies and Legislative Troubles

Under the Articles of Confederation, Congress did not have the power to raise an **army** directly; it could only ask for troops from the states. The problems with this arrangement were amply demonstrated by **Shay's Rebellion** in Massachusetts in 1786 and 1787. This rebellion was in part a response to the economic uncertainty by competing currencies. Under the Articles, Congress did not have the power to regulate inter-state or foreign commerce. Each state in the confederation had different tariffs and trade regulations, and no foreign countries would enter into trade agreements with a nation so disorganized. In short, the **Articles of Confederation** left America unable to maintain order at home, unable to gain respect abroad, and unable to improve its economy.

Philadelphia Convention of 1787

Although 55 delegates attended the **Philadelphia Convention of 1787**, only 39 signed the Constitution that emerged from this gathering. The attendees at the convention were exclusively rich men, but were all well-qualified to construct a new government. George Washington presided over the convention, and James Madison (the "father of the Constitution") served as secretary. The **representation** afforded to the people, as well as to states of different sizes, was a contentious issue throughout. Finally, in what is known as the **Great Compromise**, it was decided that the **lower house** (House of Representatives) would be chosen by the people, and the **upper house** (Senate) would be chosen by the state legislature. This convention also produced the **3/5 compromise**, whereby each slave was to be counted as 3/5 of a person. A 20-year moratorium was placed on the slave trade as well. Finally, it was decided at the convention that Congress should have control of commerce and tariffs.

Constitution

On September 17, 1787, the **Constitution** was presented to the people of the states. This document has three parts: a **preamble**; 7 **articles** outlining the powers and responsibilities of the 3 branches of government; and a section of **amendments**, the first ten of which are known as the **Bill of Rights**. The Constitution contains no bills of attainder, meaning that individuals cannot be denied life, liberty, and property without a trial. It does contain the concept of habeas corpus, meaning that arrested individuals must be charged with a crime within 72 hours. Federal judges are to be chosen for life, and there is an electoral college to select the president. In order to be in the House of Representatives, individuals had to be land-owning white males. The Constitution is famous for its system of **checks and balances** whereby the president can veto Congress, but Congress can override the veto with a 2/3 vote, and the courts can call the acts of either body "unconstitutional."

Ratification Process, Federalists, and Anti-Federalists

In order for the Constitution to take effect, it had to be **ratified** by ¾ of the states. The **Federalists** were those in favor of the Constitution. They were primarily wealthy men who lived along the coast and wanted the commercial protection afforded by a strong federal government. **Anti-Federalists**, on the other hand, were mainly small farmers and artisans who felt that the Constitution was not truly democratic and would erode the power both of the states and of individuals. The Anti-Federalists wanted a Constitution that allowed for annual elections, a standing army, and a Federal fortress. They also disapproved of the atheism of the document. Unfortunately for the Anti-Federalists, the superior organization of the Federalists helped the Constitution become ratified, despite the fact that most Americans were opposed to it.

History of the United States: 1790 to 1877

Geography of the Continent of North America

North America is the third largest continent in the world. It includes all the mainland of the northern landmass in the western hemisphere, as well as all the related offshore islands that lie north of the Isthmus of Panama. People often will call Canada and the United States "**Anglo-America**," and Mexico, Central America, and the Caribbean "**Middle America**." North America is bounded on the north by the Arctic Ocean, on the west by the Pacific Ocean and the Bering Sea, and on the east by the Atlantic Ocean and the Gulf of Mexico. The Gulf of Mexico is the largest body of water to indent the coast, the second-largest being the Hudson Bay. The Gulf of St. Lawrence and the Gulf of California also indent the coast of North America severely.

Coastal Islands, Highest Point, Longest River, and Other Major Rivers

There are a number of large **islands** off the coast of North America: Greenland, the Arctic Archipelago, the Greater and Lesser Antilles, the Alexander Archipelago, and the Aleutian Islands. The highest point in North America is **Mt. McKinley**, Alaska, and the lowest point is in **Death Valley**. The **Missouri-Mississippi River System** is the longest in North America; it is also the world's largest inland waterway system. Ships are able to enter the heart of the North America by means of the Saint Lawrence Seaway. Other major rivers of the North American continent are the Colorado, Mackenzie, Nelson, Rio Grande, St. Lawrence, Susquehanna, Columbia, and Yukon.

Climate of North America

The continent of North America contains every climatic zone, ranging from the tropical rain forests and savannas in the lowlands of Central America to the permanent ice caps in the middle of Greenland. In northern Canada, the climate is mostly subarctic and tundra. These are also found in northern Alaska. The two major mountain ranges of the continent affect the climate greatly. In the interior regions close to the Appalachian and Rocky Mountains, the climate and terrain is mostly semiarid and desert. These areas are largely prevented from receiving westerly winds and storms. Most of North America, however, has a temperate climate and is hospitable to settlement and agriculture.

Physiography of North America

North America can be divided into five regions. The **Canadian Shield** is an area of stable, ancient rock that occupies the northeast corner of the continent, including Greenland. The **Appalachian Mountains** are an old and worn-down mountain system extending from the Gaspe Peninsula to Alabama. The **Atlantic-Gulf Coastal Plain** is a stretch of lowlands running from New England to Mexico. The **Interior Lowlands** extend from central Canada to the Gulf Coast. The **North American Cordillera** is a mountain system that includes both the Pacific Margin and the Rocky Mountains. Another lesser formation, the **Transverse Volcanic Range**, extends below Mexico City.

Native Americans

Native Americans of the Northwest Coast Area

The main Native American tribes in the Northwest Coast are the **Kwakiutl**, **Haida**, and **Nootka**. These people lived in a densely forested area, with a temperate climate and heavy rainfall, and they survived mainly on salmon. The Native Americans in this region built their houses out of wood, and made canoes from cedar. These tribes built totem poles in their permanent winter villages which were elaborately carved with the faces of the tribal animal gods. They had a strict social hierarchy, with chiefs, nobles, commoners, and slaves. The Native Americans of the Pacific Northwest would be largely untouched by Europeans until the 18th century, when **fur trappers** began to encroach upon their territory.

Native Americans of the Plains Area

The Plains area extends from barely north of the Canadian border to Texas. Before the arrival of Columbus, the tribes in this region were either nomadic or sedentary. The **sedentary** tribes settled in the great river valleys and grew corn, squash, and beans. The **nomads**, meanwhile, moved their goods around on sleds pulled by dogs. They hunted buffalo by driving them into enclosures or by herding them with fires. There was also a fair amount of trade with the sedentary tribes. Many Native American tribes migrated into the Plains region; among them were the **Sioux**, **Comanche**, **Kiowa**, **Navajo**, and **Apache**. The tribes were typically governed by a chief, who would eventually be supplanted in a violent coup.

Native Americans of the Plateau Area

The Plateau area runs from just above the Canadian border into the American southwest. Some of the larger tribes in the region were the **Spokane**, **Nez Perce**, and **Shoshone**. The area where these tribes dwelled was not especially hospitable, so they spent much of their time trying to eke out a living. The tribes in the south gathered fruits and nuts, and hunted small animals. The tribes in the north fished for salmon and gathered roots and berries. Later on, these tribes would begin to hunt buffalo. Many of the northern tribes had permanent winter villages, most of which were along waterways. They borrowed the architecture of the tepee from the Plains Indians, though some tribes had long houses covered with bark.

Native Americans of the Eastern Woodlands

The Eastern Woodlands extend from the Mississippi River east to the Atlantic Ocean. The tribes of this region included the **Natchez**, **Choctaw**, **Cherokee**, and **Creek**. The people of the northeast region mostly farmed and hunted deer. They used canoes made of birch bark. The people in the Iroquois family of tribes lived either in dome-shaped wigwams or in long houses, and would typically wear clothing made from the skin of deer, often painting their faces. In the southern part of the Eastern Woodlands, there were semi-nomadic tribes who survived by hunting, fishing, and gathering. These people hunted with a bow and arrow or with a blowgun. They developed highly detailed pottery and surrounded their villages with elaborate defenses.

Native Americans Who Inhabited the Region Now Known as Canada

The Native Americans that inhabited the region now known as Canada included the **Chippewa**. This region was not especially hospitable to life and therefore there was little farming. Instead, the tribes hunted, gathered, fished, and trapped in order to survive. There were many groups of nomadic hunters who moved around from season to season. Caribou was the most popular game, and people would make all kinds of products out of parts of the animal, including caribou shoes, caribou nets, and caribou bags. These people relied on snowshoes to allow them to move quickly and without falling into icy lakes. Many of the tribes in this region had a shaman, a mystic who provided spiritual guidance to the members of the tribe.

Native Americans of the Southwest Area

The Southwest area extends across Arizona, New Mexico, Colorado, and Utah. A seminomadic people known as the **Basket Makers** hunted with the atlatl, a device that made it possible to throw a spear accurately over a great distance. The tribes in this area lived in pit dwellings which were partly underground. Later, ancestors of the Pueblo Indians would develop community houses set into the side of cliffs and canyons. These **cliff dwellings** often had a ceremonial fire pit, or kiva. These people grew corn, beans, squash, cotton, and tobacco, they killed rabbits with a wooden stick, and they traded their textiles to nomadic tribes for buffalo meat. The tribes of the Southwest also had a complex mythology and religious system.

Beginning of the Federalist Period and the Judiciary Act of 1789

After the ratification of the Constitution, **George Washington** was inaugurated as the first **president** in New York City. He immediately went outside the Constitution to form the first **Cabinet**: Thomas Jefferson, Secretary of State; Alexander Hamilton, Secretary of the Treasury; Henry Knox, Secretary of War; Edmund Randolph, Attorney General; and Samuel Osgood, Postmaster General. With the **Judiciary Act of 1789**, it was decided that there would be 6 justices and one chief justice on the Supreme Court. This act also established the federal court system and the policy of judicial review, whereby federal courts made sure that state courts and laws did not violate the Constitution. This policy was inspired by the case **Chisholm v. Georgia**, in which the Supreme Court ruled that a citizen of South Carolina could sue the state of Georgia, and that the case must be heard in a Georgia state court.

Hamilton's Funding and Economic Plan for the Financial System

The United States was born with $80 million in debt. **Alexander Hamilton**, however, was not terribly concerned by this; on the contrary, he encouraged **credit** as a means of financing the rapid capital improvements that would aid economic expansion. Hamilton introduced a **funding process**, whereby the government would buy back government bonds at full price in order to place money into the economy. Unfortunately, word of this plan leaked to some speculators, who bought the bonds at reduced rates and made huge profits. This led to accusations of a conspiracy. Another aspect of Hamilton's economic plan was for the federal government to **assume state debts**. This was done in part to tie state governments to the national government.

Custom Duties, Excise Taxes, and Federal Banks

In order to pay off the national debt, Hamilton promoted the **Revenue Act of 1789**, which was ostensibly a tax on imports, though it amounted to very little. Hamilton hoped to appease American industry with this measure without alienating foreign interests. The **Whiskey Tax**, instituted in 1791, was another attempt to generate revenue. This tax was wildly unpopular, however, and Washington was forced to call in several state militias to deal with various uprisings. At this time, Hamilton was also trying to establish a national bank, based upon the Bank of England. The **Bank of America** was established with $10 million in capital and aimed to repay foreign debts, provide a uniform national currency, aid in the collection of taxes, make loans, and act as a federal depository.

Foreign Diplomacy Under Washington

The United States stayed **neutral** during the wars of the French Revolution, even issuing a proclamation to that effect in 1793. Meanwhile, the British were constantly testing this neutrality: they did not leave their posts in the Northwest; they seized American ships and forced American sailors into service; and they frequently aided the Native Americans in their conflicts with the United States. This conflict eventually led to the **Jay Treaty** in 1794 which made the Spanish fear an Anglo-American alliance, causing them to become more willing to discuss American use of the

Mississippi River. **Pinckney's Treaty**, also known as the **Treaty of San Lorenzo** (1795), gave the United States free use of both the Mississippi and the city of New Orleans.

Review Video: Pinckney's Treaty
Visit mometrix.com/academy and enter code: 866670

Jay Treaty

The Jay Treaty of 1794 aimed to calm the post-revolution conflicts between Britain and the United States. In it, the British promised to leave their forts in the northwest and to pay for all the recent damages to ships. The British also allowed the US to form a limited commercial treaty with the British West Indies. The **Jay Treaty** asserted that the rivers and lakes of North America could be used by both Britain and the United States. However, the treaty made no provisions for any future seizures of American ships, and made no mention of Native American attacks on the American frontier. The Southern states were annoyed that the treaty won no compensation for slaves freed during the Revolutionary War, and, moreover, stipulated that Southerners had to repay their pre-war debts. The controversy surrounding the Jay Treaty led to the formation of the first **political parties**.

Rise of the First Political Parties

Unlike a faction, which exists in order to achieve a single goal, a **political party** endures beyond the accomplishment of a specific goal. The first two political parties in the United States were the **Federalists** and the **Democratic-Republicans**. **Hamilton** is the primary figure associated with the Federalists, who were wealthy northeasterners in support of a strong central government and a loose interpretation of the Constitution. The Federalists advocated a strong president, the economic policies implemented by Hamilton, and a strong relationship with the British. The Democratic-Republicans, on the other hand, were associated with the so-called "common man" of the South and West. Led by **Jefferson** and **Madison**, they advocated a strong central government, a strict interpretation of the Constitution, a close relationship with France, and closely-restricted government spending.

Washington's Farewell Address and Presidential Accomplishments

In 1796, Washington decided he was too tired to continue as president. In his famous **Farewell Address**, he implored the United States to avoid three things: permanent alliances; political factions; and sectionalism. Washington felt that the nation could only be successful if people placed the nation ahead of their own region. For his own part, Washington made some significant improvements during his presidency. He avoided war at a time when the nation was vulnerable. He also avoided political alliances and promoted the national government without alienating great numbers of people. Washington oversaw Hamilton's creation of the economic system and guided expansion to the West (as well as the creation of three new states: Vermont, Kentucky, and Tennessee).

Election of Adams and Conflict with the French

John Adams became the second president of the United States in the election of 1796; his opponent, **Thomas Jefferson**, became vice president because he received the second-most electoral votes. Adams was immediately confronted by the French, who were angry about the **Jay Treaty** and the broken **Treaty of Alliance of 1778**. After the French began destroying American ships, Adams sent American diplomats to meet with the French ambassador **Talleyrand**, who demanded tribute and then snubbed the Americans. There followed an undeclared naval war between 1798 and 1800. During which, the American military grew rapidly, warships were built and the Department of the Navy was established. Finally, at the **Convention of 1800**, the Treaty of Alliance of 1778 was torn up and it was agreed in this new **Treaty of Mortefontaine** that the Americans would pay for damages done to their ships by the French, among a host of other clauses including each country giving the other Most Favored Nation trade status.

> **Review Video: John Adams as President**
> Visit mometrix.com/academy and enter code: 156316

Domestic Events Under Adams

The Alien and Sedition Acts were established in 1798, in part because of xenophobia arising from conflict with the French. The **Alien Act** increased the number of years before one could obtain citizenship, gave the president the power to deport anyone and allowed the president to jail dangerous aliens during times of war. The **Sedition Act** made it a crime to libel or slander US officials or policies; many people believed this policy was a violation of First Amendment rights. The **Virginia and Kentucky Resolves**, promoted by Jefferson and Madison, stated that a contact exists between the state and national governments, but that the national government had exceeded its authority and broken the contract. This document advocated that states should have the power of nullification over national policies; only Virginia and Kentucky supported this policy, which had the potential to fatally undermine the Constitution.

> **Review Video: The Alien and Sedition Acts**
> Visit mometrix.com/academy and enter code: 633780

Ch 7

Election of 1800

In the election of 1800, the **Federalists** were represented by John Adams and C.C. Pinckney, and the **Democratic-Republicans** by Thomas Jefferson and Aaron Burr. The Federalists had been weakened both by the unpopularity of the Alien and Sedition Acts and the internal feud between Adams and Hamilton. They therefore focused their campaign on Jefferson, accusing him of being an atheist, of stealing money from the poor and of having an affair with a slave. In the election, Jefferson finished with the same number of electoral votes as his supposed running mate, Burr, who surprisingly refused to concede. This situation led to the **12th amendment**, which states that a candidate must stipulate his desired office. **Jefferson** finally won the tie-breaking vote in the House of Representatives, sweeping the Federalists out of office.

> **Review Video: The Election of 1800**
> Visit mometrix.com/academy and enter code: 992318

Federalist Period

The Federalist period had some remarkable successes and some bitter failures. It saw the establishment of the national bank and the Treasury system under Hamilton. The United States, amazingly, was able to pay off all of its debt during this period. The **Federalist administration** can also be credited with maintaining international neutrality, establishing the Pinckney Treaty, crushing the Whiskey Rebellion, and getting the British out of their northwest posts. On the other hand, over time the Federalists became known as an elitist party, and the Alien and Sedition Acts were very unpopular. The Jay Treaty was seen as a diplomatic failure by most Americans, and in general the Federalists were not able to maintain very cordial relations with Europe (especially France).

Jeffersonian Republicans

After using his inauguration speech to try to pacify angry Federalists, Thomas Jefferson went on to introduce the "**spoils system**," replacing Federalist office-holders with **Republicans**. He also reversed many of the Federalist policies: the Alien Act was repealed, and the Sedition Act expired in 1801 (everyone arrested under its authority was pardoned, absolved, and had their fines repaid). Jefferson also sought to reform the judiciary. The **Judiciary Act of 1801**, otherwise known as the **Circuit Court Act**, was passed by the Federalists in order to cement some of their judges in place; Jefferson in turn forced through the **Judiciary Act of 1802**, which removed all 42 of these judges.

> **Review Video: Jefferson and the Spoils System**
> Visit mometrix.com/academy and enter code: 514178

Marbury v. Madison

William Marbury was one of the Federalist judges removed from office by the Judiciary Act of 1802. Marbury, having been promised a job, brought up the issue with **James Madison**, who pleaded ignorance. The issue became contentious and in 1803 came before the Supreme Court as **Marbury v. Madison**. Although Section XIII of the Judiciary Act of 1789 had a **Writ of Mandamus** which required Madison to honor the appointment, Chief Justice **John Marshall** declared this section unconstitutional. This was a historic act: although the power of the Supreme Court to declare state and local measures unconstitutional had been established, this had never before been done on the national level. Marshall thereby established an independent judiciary; he is quoted as saying, "The Constitution is the supreme Law of the Land, with the Supreme Court as the final interpreter."

> **Review Video: Marbury v. Madison**
> Visit mometrix.com/academy and enter code: 573964

Yazoo Claims and John Randolph

In 1795, the corrupt Georgia legislature sold some land known as the **Yazoo Claims** for almost nothing to a group of northeastern speculators in exchange for a bribe. When a new group of legislators came into office in 1797, they revoked the land sales, infuriating the speculators. In 1802, the land claims were ceded to the national government and Jefferson decided to grant the speculators a cash settlement. **John Randolph**, however, was the chairman of the House committee responsible for paying this settlement, and he refused to make the payment, stating that the deal was "bathed in corruption." Though the Supreme Court eventually granted the settlements in the case **Fletcher v. Peck** (1810), Randolph was permanently alienated from Jefferson and went on to form a group called the **Tertium Quids**. This group was the ultra-conservative pro-states' rights contingent of the Democratic-Republicans.

> **Review Video: Fletcher v Peck**
> Visit mometrix.com/academy and enter code: 652746

Treaty of Ildefonso and the Louisiana Purchase

In an agreement between the French and Spanish known alternately as the **Treaty of Ildefonso** or the **Retrocession**, Napoleon Bonaparte acquired Louisiana. This, along with Spain's closing of New Orleans to American business, made Jefferson nervous, and he thus sent James Monroe to France in order to purchase New Orleans and West Florida. Bonaparte, himself made anxious by a rebellion in Haiti and a renewal of hostilities with the British, signed over 800,000 square miles to the US, making the **Louisiana Purchase** the largest land acquisition without bloodshed in human history. Napoleon hoped to curry favor with the United States, in order to forestall a possible Anglo-American alliance.

Perception of the Louisiana Purchase and Acquisition of East and West Florida

The Louisiana Purchase was probably the high point of Jefferson's presidency; it was seen at home as a diplomatic victory that also avoided drawing the United States into conflict with the European powers. It destroyed the Federalist party. After the **Louisiana Purchase** was completed, explorers set out to discover just what had been bought; among these explorers were **Meriwether Lewis** and **William Clark**. Meanwhile, the United States began to make inroads into Spanish-controlled **West Florida**. In 1810, rebels attacked Baton Rouge and James Madison claimed that West Florida was now part of the US. Of course, the Spanish protested, but they were unable to reestablish themselves. In 1818, Andrew Jackson would lead a group of soldiers into **East Florida** under the pretense of taming the Seminoles. In 1819, the Spanish would reluctantly sign the **Treaty of Onis**, in which the US formally acquired East Florida for $5 million, which the Spanish promptly returned to pay off some of their debt to the US.

Aaron Burr

After losing his challenge for the presidency in 1800, **Aaron Burr** was left out of the 1804 election and became embittered. He then lost a bid for the governorship of New York, in part because of the mudslinging of **Alexander Hamilton**. At this point, Burr began to toy with the idea of forming a new country in the West. Hamilton, hearing of this plan, informed Jefferson. Burr promptly challenged Hamilton to a **duel**, and in 1806 killed him at Weehawken, NJ. Burr headed west, and planned to start a new country in Louisiana and the areas controlled by Spain. Jefferson formally charged Burr with treason, but, citing executive privilege, refused to attend the trial. Burr was eventually found not guilty, in part because he had only planned a new country, and in part because the US was unable to find any reliable witnesses.

> **Review Video: Aaron Burr**
> Visit mometrix.com/academy and enter code: 273358

Foreign Policy Under the Jeffersonian Republicans

The most important event during the dominance of the Jeffersonian Republicans was the **War of 1812**, fought between France and Britain. In the United States, there was much speculation as to whether the young nation would side with the shark (Britain) or the tiger (France). In 1803, Jefferson had declared American ships neutral, an act which annoyed both sides. The British subsequently passed the **Orders-in-Council**, and the French the **Berlin and Milan Decrees**, all of which were designed to weaken American shipping in Europe. The US responded with the **Non-Importation Act of 1806**, though this was largely a failure. In 1807, an American ship called the **Chesapeake** was attacked by a British ship, leading Jefferson to issue the **Embargo Act of 1807**.

This act forbade American ships from leaving for foreign ports; it was very unpopular, and was repealed in 1809.

Review Video: Opinions about the War of 1812
Visit mometrix.com/academy and enter code: 274558

Madison and "Peaceful Coercion," and the Non-Intercourse Act of 1809

In the 1808 election, **James Madison** of the Democrat-Republicans easily defeated C.C. Pinckney. Madison continued Jefferson's policy of "**peaceful coercion**" with respect to France and Britain, but the lack of an organized American military made it difficult for him to get the attention of these major powers. In 1809, Madison convinced Congress to pass the **Non-Intercourse Act of 1809**, which forbade trade with Britain and France until they began treating American business fairly. When the British ambassador **David Erskine** vowed to improve the treatment of American businesses, Madison agreed to trade with England. However, Erskine's superior quickly overruled him, making Madison look ridiculous and souring Anglo-American relations further.

Macon's Bill No. 2

Madison replaced the Non-Intercourse Act of 1809 with **Macon's Bill No. 2**, which declared that America would be open to trade with any country. The bill also stipulated that if either Britain or France agreed to neutral trading rights with the US, the US would immediately cease trade with the other. France jumped at this opportunity, and the US cut diplomatic ties with Britain. The British, weakened by the American embargoes and by a bitter winter, rescinded the **Orders-in-council**, although the US had already declared war upon them. After the British Prime Minister was assassinated, the new foreign secretary, **Castlereagh**, tried to mend relations, but the US went to war anyway. The **War of 1812** was very unpopular, especially among Federalists in the northeast. Many Americans felt that England could not be beaten, that engaging in a war would damage US business, and that Napoleon was not a very savory ally.

War of 1812

Controversy

The conservative members of Madison's party, known as the **Tertium Quids**, opposed the **War of 1812** because they felt it would be too expensive, would result in the perpetuation of a standing army, would damage America economically, and would lead to the acquisition of Canada as a slave state. These critics were opposed in Congress by the **Warhawks**, so-called by the Federalists to imply that they were picking a fight. The Warhawks mainly represented the Southwest and the West, and included luminaries such as Henry Clay, John C. Calhoun, and Felix Grundy. They supported the war because they thought it would bolster foreign trade, would discourage the British from inciting Native Americans along the frontier, and could result in land gain. In selling the war to the American people, Madison stressed the British insult to American honor; he mentioned several stories about impressments of Americans into British military service.

Events Leading Up to Combat

Despite a great deal of bloated rhetoric both for and against the war, the US fought against Britain for a few basic reasons, namely to gain more **land** and to destroy **alliances** between the British and Native Americans. Americans had become incensed when, following his defeat to the Americans at Tippecanoe Creek, **Chief Tecumseh** had fled north into British-controlled Canada. This provocation provided enough popular support to declare war. Unfortunately, the American military was both unprepared and overconfident. Most American military strategists thought it

- 35 -

would be quite easy to take Canada, but the army had only 35,000 troops at the time. Moreover, the first Bank of the United States had just gone defunct, and so there were scarce economic resources to support a war.

Major Battles

At the **Battle of Lake Erie** in September of 1813, the American Commander Perry secured Detroit for the US. At the **Battle of Lake Champlain**, the American General Thomas McDonough secured northern New York from British invasion. At the **Battle of the Thames**, the American General William Henry Harrison defeated a coalition of British and Native American forces; Tecumseh was killed. Andrew Jackson scored a decisive victory at the **Battle of Horseshoe Bend**. During this war, much of Washington, DC (including the White House) was torched. A crucial point of the war came when the US was able to successfully defend **Fort McHenry**, outside of Baltimore; this conflict inspired Francis Scott Key's composition of "The Star-spangled Banner." At the **Battle of New Orleans**, Andrew Jackson used a rag-tag collection of soldiers and pirates to defeat the British navy.

Conclusion of the War

Throughout the War of 1812, there was loud opposition from the **Federalists** in the northeast. At the **Hartford Convention**, they formally blamed Madison for the war, and proposed changes to the Constitution whereby a 2/3 vote would be needed for declaring war and for admitting new states to the union. The War of 1812 required several agreements to fully restore relations between the US and Britain. The **Treaty of Ghent** returned Anglo-American ties to their pre-war terms, and proposed that commissions be created to settle differences. The **Rush-Bagot Treaty of 1817** formally declared that there would be no naval race between the 2 countries. At the **Convention of 1818**, a line was drawn along the 49th parallel, dividing Canada from Louisiana, and it was declared that the 2 countries would jointly occupy Oregon. In the **Adams-Onis Treaty of 1819**, a western boundary for Louisiana was set, and the Spanish renounced their claims to Oregon.

> **Review Video: The Adams-Onís Treaty**
> Visit mometrix.com/academy and enter code: 802716

Significance

The War of 1812 did not really accomplish its supposed goal of establishing neutral trading rights for American ships. The exodus of Napoleon during the war made this a moot point. Nevertheless, from Madison's perspective the war could only be seen as a major **success**. The United States lost no major territory, and scored enough victories to keep the British from making any extreme demands. More importantly, perhaps, Americans were overjoyed that the US was finally getting respect from the major European powers. **Nationalism** exploded in the US: people forgot the debacle of the failed national bank, and the economy boomed. Finally, the success of the War of 1812 effectively drove the final nail into the coffin of the **Federalist party**.

Strengthening of American National Identity

The success of the War of 1812 and the prospering economy made Madison extremely popular. In the northeast, with the implementation of the British factory system, and in the southeast, with the invention of the cotton gin, manufacturing interests were booming. This sense of **national identity** was strengthened by the emergence of the United States' first generation of **post-colonial artists**. In literature, James Fenimore Cooper and Washington Irving (*The Legend of Sleepy Hollow*) were eminent. A uniquely American style of **architecture** developed, led by Jefferson, among others, emphasizing columns, symmetry, and classical proportions. The **Hudson River school** produced a group of painters influenced by the natural beauty of their region; among them John James Audubon.

Triumph of Neo-Federalism

In 1816, Madison declared that that the government should increase the army, the national debt, and the banking interests, an agenda oddly reminiscent of Federalism. The **Second Bank of the United States** was shown to be necessary by the War of 1812, but it was poorly organized and came to be known as a "moneyed monster." The **Tariff of 1816** was established to protect fledgling industry; it was as popular in the northeast as it was unpopular in the south. Much of the tariff money went to developing infrastructure; the new method of **paving** invented by John MacAdam enabled the creation of long thoroughfares, mostly in the north. It was even proposed in the so-called "Bonus Bill" that all of the surplus money from the new bank should go to the roads; Madison vetoed this measure to avoid further alienating the south.

"The Era of Good Feelings" from 1817 to 1825

In the election of 1816, the Democrat-Republican **James Monroe** defeated the last Federalist candidate, Rufus King, by a landslide. The Federalist opposition to the War of 1812 doomed the party to extinction. Monroe's early term was not without its problems, however. A mild depression caused by over-speculation on western lands led to the **Panic of 1819**, and began a 20-year boom-bust cycle. These problems were exacerbated by the **Second Bank of the United States**; the Bank's pressure on the so-called "wildcat" banks to foreclose on properties, as well as the unwillingness of the Bank to loan money, made it very unpopular. The nationalism generated by the War of 1812 was damaged by these economic travails.

The Marshall Court (1801-1835)

The Supreme Court led by **John Marshall** is credited with increasing the power of the national government over that of the states. This court also gave the judicial branch more power and prestige, notably in the case of **Marbury v. Madison** (1803). Marshall was known as an arch-Federalist, and as a loose interpreter of the Constitution. In the case **McCullough v. Maryland** (1819), the court ruled that a national bank is allowed by the Constitution, and that states cannot tax a federal agency. In the case of **Gibbons v. Ogden** (1824), the right of Congress to regulate interstate commerce was reaffirmed, and indeed federal regulation of just about anything was made possible. In **Fletcher v. Peck** (1810), the sanctity of contracts was asserted; this case also established the right of the Supreme Court to declare state laws unconstitutional.

Monroe Doctrine

After a series of revolutions in Latin America, the United States was the first to recognize the **sovereignty** of the new countries. This was in part because the revolutionaries had used the United States as inspiration, in part because the US preferred to have weak, independent nations nearby, and in part because the US wanted to maintain and expand its lucrative trade with Latin America. The British attempted to persuade the US to sign an agreement preventing foreign intervention in Latin America, but Monroe decided to maintain American independence and issue his own document. This document, known as the **Monroe Doctrine**, had as its two main principles *non-intervention* and *non-colonization*. Many considered it a "paper tiger," because it was really

- 37 -

only as effective as the American ability to enforce it. Still, it seemed to encourage foreign nations to come to the bargaining table rather than test the American military.

Jacksonian Democracy

ch 8

The 1820s and 30s are known as the era of **Jacksonian democracy**, which was political rather than economic or social. Jackson was considered to be emblematic of the "common man." In the years after the conclusion of the War of 1812, it was generally considered that America was "safe for democracy," and thus **suffrage** was extended to poor people in many states. As more people became involved in politics, campaigning became more about image and perception than the issues. This change also ended the tradition known as "**King Caucus**," in which candidates were chosen by a small group of powerful men; now, candidates were to be selected by a series of primaries and nominating conventions. Furthermore, the members of the electoral college would be chosen by the voters rather than by the state legislature. The new system maintained the tradition of **patronage** (the spoils system), in which newly-elected officials would fill the government offices with their supporters.

Election of 1824 and Adams' Administration

All the major candidates in the 1824 election were **Democrat-Republicans**. Although Andrew Jackson received more electoral votes than **John Quincy Adams**, he did not win a majority, and Adams (with the help of Henry Clay) won the run-off in the House of Representatives. Adams was a fierce **nationalist** at a time when many in the country were sectionalist. Although his initiatives for a national university and public funding for the arts were well-meaning, Adams was still believed to be out of touch with the common man. He further alienated the middle and lower classes with the **Tariff of 1828**, known in the South as the "Tariff of Abominations." The South was already on shaky economic ground and the tariff became a scapegoat for its troubles. **John C. Calhoun** was an especially ardent Southern voice; he futilely proposed that states should have the ability to nullify federal regulations.

1828

The election of 1828 is considered the first **modern campaign** in American politics. **Andrew Jackson** had the first campaign manager, Amos Kendall, and produced buttons, posters, and slogans to support his candidacy. These men—Jackson, Kendall, John C. Calhoun, and Martin van Buren—formed the beginning of the **Democratic party**. Meanwhile, the incumbent John Quincy Adams ran a very formal campaign, with little of the "flesh-pressing" of Jackson. Adams tried to discredit Jackson as an adulterer and bigamist because Jackson's wife had not been officially divorced at the time of their marriage. When his wife died during the campaign, however, the popular sentiment returned to Jackson, and he won the election by a considerable margin. Jackson's inauguration was an over-crowded, chaotic affair; the president suffered three cracked ribs during the festivities.

Jacksonian Democracy

Andrew Jackson is often seen as a symbol of the rising power of the New West, or as an embodiment of the "rags to riches" fable. He spent much of his presidency trying to promote the idea of **nationalism** at a time when most of the country was ardently sectionalist. During his presidency, he dominated Congress, vetoing more legislation than all of the previous presidents combined. He was also famous for his so-called "**Kitchen Cabinet**," a group of close advisers without official positions. Many of these men later received formal appointments, including Secretary of State (Martin van Buren), Postmaster General (Amos Kendall), and Secretary of the Treasury (Roger B. Taney).

Major Events of the Jackson Era

Raid into Florida and the Webster-Hayne Debate

One of the least successful events in Jackson's presidency was a **raid into Florida** in 1828, made for the purpose of subduing the Seminoles. The raid did not go well, and even Jackson's Secretary of War, John C. Calhoun, referred to it as "idiotic." Another major event in Jackson's term was the **Webster-Hayne debate** of 1829-30, held to debate western expansion. The senators of the northeast were opposed to western migration, mainly because they felt it would weaken manufacturing and create a new political rival. Senator **Robert Hayne** of South Carolina blasted the war record of the Northeast, in the hopes of allying the West and the South. **Daniel Webster** (MA) retorted that the US is not a collection of states, but a union that happens to be divided into states; he asserted that if states could nullify federal measures, the only thing holding the union together was a "rope of sand."

Tariff of 1832 and the Force Act of 1832

At a feast in celebration of Thomas Jefferson—a man noted for his nationalism—Andrew Jackson promoted the idea of the nation, saying, "Our Union, it must be preserved." John C. Calhoun responded with a speech in which he referred to "Our Union, next to our liberty most dear," indicating that the South was not going to back down. The milder **Tariff of 1832** was then offered by Jackson to appease the South and Calhoun; instead, Southern politicians declared it was not enough, and Calhoun resigned from Congress in order to organize the opposition to all tariffs. Henry Clay, who realized that Jackson could easily overpower South Carolina, was further disturbed by the **Force Act of 1832**, which stated that the president had the right to use military force to keep a state in the union. So, Clay proposed an even lower **Compromise Tariff of 1833**: the tariff would be lowered from 35% to 20-25% over the next ten years. Both sides agreed to this compromise.

<u>Maysville Road Veto and Native American Removal</u>

In 1830, Jackson set a precedent by **vetoing the funding of a road** that was to be entirely within one state (Kentucky). Many believed that Jackson vetoed this bill to spite Henry Clay, but the move had some positive political consequences as well: the Southerners appreciated the idea that states should tend to their own business and northerners liked it because the road would have given people easier access to the West. Jackson's attempts at **relocating Native Americans** were less successful. The passage of the **Indian Resettlement Act of 1830** was the first attempt by the national government to force migration. In the case of **Worcester v. Georgia** (1832), the Supreme Court ruled against those who sought to grab Native lands. John Marshall asserted that the **Cherokee nation** was sovereign, but a ward of the US. Despite Marshall's assertion of Native American rights, Jackson supported the slow and steady conquest of land in the South and West.

<u>Bank War of 1836</u>

It had already been arranged that the **renewal of the Second Bank of America** would be discussed in 1836. It was common knowledge that Jackson hated the Bank, and thus Henry Clay and others tried to renew it ahead of time, in 1832. Jackson was then forced to assert his position: he declared that the bank was anti-West, anti-American, unconstitutional and a "monopoly of money." The unpopularity of Clay's attempt to renew the Bank was a main reason that he was crushed by Jackson in the 1832 election. After making sure that the Bank would not be renewed, Jackson sought to mend fences with the Northeast by avidly promoting the Union. This was Jackson's genius as a politician; he always was careful to get what he wanted without fully alienating any faction.

Election of 1836 and the Van Buren Presidency

When Jackson decided not to pursue a third term as president, his vice president **Martin Van Buren** ran and won over a group of challengers including the Whig candidate William Henry Harrison. Van Buren's presidency was marked by frequent border disputes with Canada. Also, Van Buren suffered through the **Panic of 1837**; like in 1819, this was caused by over-speculation in the West. In the 1836 "Specie Circular," Jackson had declared that all land bought from the government must be paid for in gold coins. Because gold was hard to come by, many people lost their property. Further economic problems were created by over-spending on infrastructure in many states. One of the results of Van Buren's handling of the situation was that it became acceptable for the president to influence the amount of money in circulation. In 1840, a listless Van Buren was defeated by **Harrison**, who promptly died after a month as president. **John Tyler** became the next president.

Tyler Presidency

John Tyler, a Virginia aristocrat, was the first vice president to take over in mid-term. Oddly, even though he was the Whig candidate, he opposed almost all of the Whig agenda. Henry Clay hoped to dominate Tyler, but his attempts to create a third national bank and to improve infrastructure in the West were both vetoed by Tyler. Tyler's presidency was also fraught with conflict with the British; he endured the **Lumberjacks' War of 1842** and the **Hunters' Lodges skirmishes** in 1838, both of which were minor conflicts along the Canadian border. There was also the incident of the *Caroline*, an American ship sunk by the British for allegedly smuggling supplies to Canadian rebels.

In the **Webster-Ashburton Treaty of 1842** fugitives were exchanged, the border of Maine was set at the St. John River and it was established that the British could no longer search American ships.

Review Video: John Tyler as President
Visit mometrix.com/academy and enter code: 791157

Expansion and Manifest Destiny

The phrase "manifest destiny," meaning the inevitability and righteousness of the American expansion westward, was coined by the editor **John O'Sullivan**. This idea was lent further credence by the work of Horace Greeley, the journalist responsible for the admonition, "Go West, young man!" Besides this mythology, however, there were some sound reasons why the United States expanded westward. For one thing, there was cheap and fertile land in the west, and the more that was claimed by the Americans, the less which could be claimed by the British. Americans also had an eye towards claiming the western ports to begin trading with Asia. Finally, many Americans felt that they would only be benefiting the world by spreading their ideals of liberty and democracy across as much land as possible.

Review Video: Manifest Destiny
Visit mometrix.com/academy and enter code: 957409

Texas' Role in US Expansion

In 1821, **Mexico** received its independence from Spain. Mexico sold Texan lands to Americans, yet these people were still required to live under Mexican civil law (for one thing, people had to convert to Catholicism). In 1832, however, **Santa Anna** led a coup in Mexico and decided to crack down on the Texans. This led to the **Texas Revolution of 1836**, in which Texan General William Travis' men were massacred by the forces of Santa Anna at the **Alamo**, in which both Davy Crockett and Jim Bowie were killed. After suffering some other defeats the Texans, led by Sam Houston, finally defeated Santa Anna at the **Battle of San Jacinto** in 1836 and he was forced below the Rio Grande. Nevertheless, Texas was not made part of the US, mainly because the issue of slavery was so contentious at the time.

US Expansion Including Salt Lake City, Oregon, and California

The territory of **Oregon** became more important to the US government as fur-trapping became a lucrative industry. Oregon was also known to contain rich farmland. As for **California**, its natural bounty had been described by whalers since the 1820s. In the 1840s, whole families (including the ill-fated Donner party) began to migrate there. Around this time the **Church of Jesus Christ of Latter-day Saints**, otherwise known as the Mormon Church, was founded by Joseph Smith. Among the beliefs espoused by the Mormons were polygamy, communalism and the abolition of slavery. After Smith's death, the Mormons were led by Brigham Young and settled in what is now **Salt Lake City**. Meanwhile, in 1848 gold was discovered in a California stream, generating still more excitement over the economic potential of the West.

Presidency of James K. Polk

The election of 1844 brought to the forefront a number of critical issues; the economy was still hurting from the Panic of 1837, there was growing support for abolitionism and the issue of manifest destiny was gaining steam. Somewhat surprisingly, the bland North Carolinian **James K. Polk** defeated Henry Clay and succeeded John Tyler as president. He instituted the **Walker Tariff**, which lowered the rate at which foreign goods were taxed from 35% to 25%. He also reinstated the **Independent Sub-Treasury system** in 1846. Mainly, however, Polk's presidency is associated with westward expansion; **Texas** was brought into the union as a slave state in December of 1845. Polk also spent considerable time trying to get possession of Oregon.

> **Review Video: James K. Polk as President**
> Visit mometrix.com/academy and enter code: 917254

Mexican War

Causes

The immediate causes of the **Mexican War** were the American annexation of Texas, disputes over the Southern border of Texas and the large amount of money owed to the United States by Mexico. Moreover, it was well known that the Mexicans held the US in contempt, considering them greedy land-grabbers. **Polk** sent an emissary to buy Texas, California, and some Mexican territory for $30 million; he was refused. **Zachary Taylor** then led an American expedition into a disputed area of Texas where some of them were killed. Polk was able to use these deaths as a rationale for war, despite considerable opposition in Congress. Overall, the Democrats supported the war, while the Whigs, led in part by Abraham Lincoln, were opposed.

Major Battles and Conclusion of War

The United States scored major victories over Mexico at **Buena Vista**, where they were led by Zachary Taylor, and **Vera Cruz**, where they were led by Winfield Scott. The American effort in New Mexico was led by Stephen Kearney and in California by John C. Fremont. The **Treaty of Guadalupe-Hidalgo** was signed in 1848 after Polk sent an emissary with cash in an effort to persuade Santa Anna to stop the war. Under the terms of the treaty, the US got California, the rest of Texas, and all of the Mexican territory between Louisiana and California (including what would become Utah and Nevada). In exchange, the US erased a good deal of Mexico's debts. Controversy immediately erupted over whether the new territories would be allowed to have slaves; some abolitionists wanted to cancel the treaty while some Southern Democrats wanted to claim the entirety of Mexico.

Road to Civil War

There was immense controversy surrounding the **slavery policy** in the new American territories after the war with Mexico: Polk wanted to simply extend the line of the **Missouri Compromise** out to the Pacific while abolitionists offered the **Wilmot Proviso**, which declared that none of the territories should have slaves. The Southern states felt slavery should be allowed, and a more moderate view was offered by Stephen Douglas, who declared that the people of the new states should decide whether they wanted slavery or not. In the election of 1848, the war-hero **Zachary Taylor** (Whig) defeated Lewis Cass (Democrat) and the former president Martin Van Buren (Free Soil party, a collection of abolitionist interests).

> **Review Video: Missouri Compromise**
> Visit mometrix.com/academy and enter code: 848091

Gold Rush and the Compromise of 1850

After **Zachary Taylor** won the election of 1848, he immediately had to deal with the issue of slavery in the new western territories. This issue was magnified by the California gold rush. Taylor declared that all of the lands would be free, enraging the Southerners. Soon after, however, Taylor died of food poisoning and was succeeded by Vice-president **Millard Fillmore**. In order to solve the problem of slavery in the west, Henry Clay proposed the so-called **Compromise of 1850**: California would be a free state, while New Mexico would be allowed to decide for itself; there would be no more slave trading in the District of Columbia; there would be tighter laws regarding fugitive slaves; and Texas would receive $10 million for its lost territories. Fillmore readily signed this agreement, but problems with it arose immediately. One of which was that the **Underground Railroad** of **Harriet Tubman** was already making it very difficult to catch fugitive slaves.

Election of 1852 and the Growing Crisis of Slavery

In the election of 1852, Democrat **Franklin Pierce** easily defeated the Whig Winfield Scott who was hurt by his association with the abolitionist William H. Seward. At this time, despite the growing crisis of slavery, there were some positive changes in the US. One was that the introduction of **California** as a free state permanently upset the sectional balance. Immigration into the Northeastern cities was bringing a wealth of new ideas. The northern states resisted the fugitive slave laws by passing initiatives in support of personal liberties and by aiding the Underground Railroad. Harriet Beecher Stowe enraged the South with her novel Uncle Tom's Cabin (1852). In 1857, Hinton R. Helper published "The Impending Crisis of the South," an essay that suggested the South was becoming a slave to the North because of its reactionary view on slavery.

Trans-Continental Railroad, Ostend Manifesto, and Kansas-Nebraska Act

The construction of the Trans-Continental Railroad was begun in 1853 for the purpose of transporting easterners to California. With the **Gadsden Purchase**, the US had purchased some New Mexican lands so that the train could avoid the mountains. With the **Ostend Manifesto** in 1854, the US attempted to purchase Cuba from Spain for $120 million; Spain refused, and though the US threatened to take the island by force, they never did (in part because it was believed that the South wanted to make it a slave state). The **Kansas-Nebraska Act** (1854), authored by Stephen Douglas, divided the Nebraska territory into two parts (Kansas and Nebraska) and declared that slavery would be determined by popular sovereignty in those territories. This act drove northerners to the liberal side and caused the creation of the **Republican party**. The opposing factions engaged in violence to try and win the popular vote. Though Kansas worded its constitution in an attempt to have slaves, the document fell apart upon review by Congress, and Kansas entered as a free state.

Sumner-Brooks Incident, Election of 1856, and the Dred Scott Case

In 1856, Senator **Charles Sumner** (MA) gave an impassioned speech on the "Crime against Kansas," in which he blamed the south for the violence. One of the men whom he singled out for blame was the uncle of Senator **Preston Brooks** (SC); Brooks beat Sumner with his walking stick, and was glorified in the South. In the election of 1856, **James Buchanan** (Democrat) defeated several candidates, including Millard Fillmore (American party; some southern states had threatened to secede should Fillmore prevail). Next came the **Dred Scott** case. Scott was a slave taken to a free state by his owner, and then transported back to a slave state. Abolitionists said he should be a free man. The Supreme Court, however, ruled that slaves are property and can be transported across state lines without being changed. This decision effectively rendered the Kansas-Nebraska Act, the Missouri Compromise, and the whole idea of popular sovereignty unconstitutional.

> **Review Video: Dred Scott Act**
> Visit mometrix.com/academy and enter code: 364838

Lincoln-Douglas Debates and John Brown's Raid

During the campaign to become senator of Illinois in 1858, **Abraham Lincoln** and **Stephen Douglas** eloquently debated the issue of slavery. In the so-called **Freeport Doctrine**, Lincoln questioned whether the people of a territory could vote against slavery. The Supreme Court would say no, but Lincoln wondered whether the people should not have the final say. Douglas essentially agreed, stating that the people of the territory should decide. Douglas won the election, though his stance on slavery irritated Southerners. In 1859, the abolitionist **John Brown** led a raid on a federal arsenal at Harper's Ferry, Virginia. Brown's group was only able to take a fire station, and Brown himself was captured and executed by a battalion led by **Robert E. Lee**. Brown became a martyr to the North.

Election of 1860 and Secession of the South

In the election of 1860, **Abraham Lincoln** defeated three other challengers. Lincoln's platform was anti-slavery, though he vowed to leave it intact where it already existed. He also promised full rights to immigrants, the completion of a Pacific Railroad, free homesteads, and a protective tariff. After the election, South Carolina **seceded**, followed by the rest of the Deep South (Mississippi, Alabama, Georgia, Louisiana, Florida and Texas). These states established the **Confederate States of America**, with its capital in Montgomery, Alabama. The president of the CSA was **Jefferson Davis**. Outgoing US President Buchanan claimed that he had no constitutional authority to stop the secession, but upon entering office Lincoln attempted to maintain control of all Southern forts. This led to the firing on **Ft. Sumter** (SC) by the Confederates. As Lincoln called for aid, the Upper South (Virginia, Arkansas, North Carolina and Tennessee) seceded as well, and the CSA made Richmond, Virginia its new capital.

> **Review Video:** The Civil War: Abraham Lincoln and Secession
> Visit mometrix.com/academy and enter code: 570281

Compromises to Save the Union

The US government made a number of compromises in an attempt to preserve the Union after Lincoln's election. The **Crittenden Compromise** extended the line of the Missouri Compromise and promised federal protection of slavery south of that line. The **House of Representatives Compromise** offered an extension of the Missouri Compromise and a Constitutional amendment to protect slavery. The **Virginia Peace Convention** produced an offer to extend the line of the Missouri Compromise and establish that slavery can never be outlawed except by the permission of the owner. Finally, Congress offered $300 for each slave. The South said that this was not enough money and the North was appalled by the offer, regardless.

Civil War

The Civil War was fought for a number of reasons, but the most important of these was the controversy about **slavery**. The issue of slavery touched on moral, economic, and political themes. Also, the differing geography of the North and South had caused the latter to develop an **economy** that they felt could only survive through slavery. The Civil War also sprang from the ongoing debate over **states' rights**; many in the South felt that states should have the power to nullify federal regulations and believed that the North had too much representation in Congress; and, indeed, the North had received much more federal aid for infrastructure. Finally, there was a general difference in **culture** between the North and South; the North was more of a dynamic and democratic society, while the South was more of a static oligarchy.

Advantages of the North

The **Northern side** in the Civil War contained 22 states with 22 million people. The North also contained most of the US' coal, iron, and copper, as well as 92% of the industry. The Union side had more than twice as much railroad track as the Confederacy and a vastly larger navy. Most importantly, perhaps, the Union had a huge advantage in **troops**. Most of the Northern troops were either volunteers or had been conscripted (starting in 1863). It was permissible to pay someone to take your space in the military. The North generally had between 2 and 3 times as many troops as the South during the war. The South was really only able to survive for so long because it fought a very defensive war.

Advantages and Disadvantages of the Confederacy

The **Confederate States of America** was comprised of 11 states with only 9 million people. When the war began, the South had no organized army or navy. At first, the troops were strictly volunteers, but eventually the CSA established a draft to bolster the ranks. The Confederacy did have some advantages, however. One was that they were fighting on their own soil and thus they already had interior lines of defense as well as knowledge of the terrain. On the whole, the Confederate commanders were more experienced and talented. Finally, the Confederacy had a psychological advantage over the North: they were fighting for a **tangible reason** (namely, to preserve their lives and property, while the North had to motivate its troops with notions of "preserving the Union."

Military Strategies of the North and South

The North began the Civil War by trying to **blockade** the Southern coast and seal off the border states; they hoped to end the war quickly by preventing supplies from reaching the Confederacy. The North also wanted to divide the South into two parts by seizing control of the Mississippi River. This plan would later be adjusted, and **Sherman's March** would try to divide the South into a northern and southern half. The Confederacy, meanwhile, knew that its best chance for success was to fight **defensively** (the South did not want any Northern territory). They also knew that they would need help from European powers. The South hoped to outlast the North's will to fight, to capture Washington, DC, and to receive Maryland into the Confederacy.

Major Battles

First Bull Run, Shiloh, and Second Bull Run: The **First Battle of Bull Run** was fought in Manassas, VA in July of 1861. The North believed that an easy victory here would allow them to quickly take Richmond. Washingtonians even picnicked around the battlefield, anticipating a pleasant spectacle. It was not to be, however: led by Stonewall Jackson (who actually earned that nickname at this battle), the South won a shocking victory. As a result, the South became somewhat overconfident, and the North realized it was in for a long war. At the **Battle of Shiloh** (TN) in April of 1862, Ulysses S. Grant led the Union to its first major victory. At the **Second Battle of Bull Run** in August of 1862, Stonewall Jackson again defeated a Northern army, this time with the help of Robert E. Lee.

> **Review Video: Robert E. Lee**
> Visit mometrix.com/academy and enter code: 637719

Antietam: At the **Battle of Antietam** (MD) in September of 1862, the Confederate General Robert E. Lee went on the offensive, hoping to bring Maryland into the Confederacy, sever the channels between Washington, DC and the North, and attract the recognition of the European powers. This was the bloodiest battle of the Civil War and ended in a draw. It was after this battle that Lincoln issued his famous **Emancipation Proclamation**. This document freed the slaves in any area that was taken by the Union, or in areas from which slaves could enter the Union. It did not, however, free slaves in the Border States, because Lincoln wanted to maintain loyalty to the Union in these areas. The aims of the Emancipation Proclamation were three: to keep the British from assisting the South, to motivate the Northern troops and to effect a positive moral change.

Fredericksburg, Chancellorsville, and Gettysburg: At the **Battle of Fredericksburg** (VA) in December of 1862, Robert E. Lee successfully repelled the attacks of the Union General Burnside. At the **Battle of Chancellorsville** (VA) in May of 1863, Lee scored his greatest victory of the war; it was during this battle, however, that the Confederate General Stonewall Jackson was mortally wounded by his own troops. At the **Battle of Gettysburg** (PA) in July of 1863, the Confederacy troops led by Lee suffered a damaging defeat. Lee had hoped to take some pressure off the South with a successful surge into the North, but instead got caught in an unfavorable tactical position and endured massive casualties. Most historians believe the Union victory at Gettysburg was the turning point in the war.

Vicksburg, Atlanta, and Sherman's March: The Union General mounted a siege against the crucial Confederate city of **Vicksburg** (MS) in July of 1863. When the Confederates had finally been starved into surrender, the Union had total control of the Mississippi River. Then, between July and October of 1864, the major Southern rail hub of **Atlanta** was conquered and burned by Union troops under General William Sherman. This victory guaranteed that Lincoln would be reelected in the election of 1864. It also marked the beginning of **Sherman's March to the Sea**, a campaign of devastation mounted by the Union in late 1864 and early 1865. Sherman's troops melted Southern rails and destroyed Southern crops and factories, creating a swath of chaos that stretched from Atlanta to Savannah.

Election of 1876 and Compromise of 1877

In 1876, **Rutherford B. Hayes** (Republican) defeated Samuel Tilden (Democrat) after an electoral commission composed mostly of Republicans ruled that certain votes by carpet-bag governments should have gone to him. As part of the ensuing **Compromise of 1877**, the South was given federal money for improvements to infrastructure, a Southerner was placed in Hayes' Cabinet, and the Union troops propping up the carpetbag governments were removed. This election established the tradition of the "**Solid South**": it was assumed that every year the majority of Southerners would vote for the Democratic candidate.

New South in the 1880s

In the 1880s, the old Southern plantations began to break up, in part because the high taxes imposed by the new governments made them unprofitable. The land was mainly worked by tenant farmers and sharecroppers: **tenant farmers** worked and paid rent on someone else's land, while **sharecroppers** worked the whole plantation and got a share of the crop. Tenant farmers were mostly poor whites, while sharecroppers were mostly freed blacks. There was considerable diversification in agriculture around this time, brought on not only by innovation (cotton picker, tractor), but by the **Morrill Land Grant Act**, which gave grants for the creation of agricultural colleges. Clarence Birdseye's development of the refrigerated railroad car spurred farming as well. Also, as the road and rail infrastructure improved in the South, so did Southern industry.

Redeemers

The Redeemers sought to prevent blacks from voting and to return power to the "natural leaders." In response, the **Populist party** was formed; it was an uneasy alliance of blacks and poor whites. Southern Democrats tried to exploit the tension within the Populist party. In order to keep blacks from voting, Democrats subjected voters to literacy tests, property tests, criminal background checks, residency requirements and the so-called **Grandfather Clause**, which stated that individuals could not vote unless their ancestors had voted before January 1, 1867. These restrictions, known collectively as the **Mississippi Plan**, were actually upheld by the Supreme Court, which ruled in **Williams v. Mississippi** (1898) that they were legal because they never explicitly stated that blacks could not vote.

Black Southerners and Segregation

Most Southern Democrats supported **segregation**, or the separation of the races. Although the **Civil Rights Act of 1875** had outlawed segregated restaurants and hotels, among other things, the Supreme Court ruled in 1883 that this act violated the 14th amendment because only states, and not individuals, could be forbidden from segregation. The **Jim Crow laws** were those rules that segregated blacks and whites. Although de facto (by custom) segregation had existed in the North for years, the South began to implement segregation de jure (by law). In **Plessy v. Ferguson** (1896), the Supreme Court ruled that accommodations should be "separate but equal." In **Cummings v. Board of Education** (1898), the Supreme Court allowed public schools to be segregated.

Booker T. Washington and W.E.B. DuBois

Booker T. Washington was an ex-slave who founded the Tuskegee Institute; he felt that blacks should establish economic independence before worrying about political rights. In his **Atlanta Exposition speech**, he declared that blacks needed to humble themselves to whites. Professor **W.E.B. DuBois** attacked Washington's speech as a compromise; DuBois believed blacks should take everything they were due. In 1914, both Washington and DuBois met with Marcus Garvey, who believed that blacks should return to Africa and establish a separate country (interestingly, most of Garvey's financial support came from the KKK). At around this time, Paul Laurence Dunbar was achieving renown as the "poet laureate of the Negro race," and Charles Waddell Chestnut was admired as a popular black novelist.

> **Review Video: Susan B. Anthony, Robert Lafollette, and W.E.B. DuBois**
> Visit mometrix.com/academy and enter code: 989776

Subordination of Western Native Americans Until 1874

The Native Americans who roamed the Great Plains were known as fierce hunters and there were a few bloody encounters between settlers heading west and the natives. In 1851, the US established the **Concentration policy**, which encouraged Native Americans to live close to one another. This strategy was untenable, however, and the period from 1860-90 was marked by frequent conflict. In the **Sioux Wars** of 1865-7, the Sioux were led by **Red Cloud**; they fought and lost to American troops after their sacred hunting ground was mined. For a while, the US tried to group tribes on reservations in Oklahoma and the Black Hills; from 1869-74, Generals Sherman and Sheridan engaged in a **War of Extermination** to kill those who refused to move.

Subordination of the Western Native Americans from 1875-1887

According to **Grant's Peace Program**, each Native American tribe would be put under the control of different religious groups. In 1875, miners were allowed back into the Black Hills, prompting the **Sioux War** of 1875-6, during which Sitting Bull defeated Custer at the **Battle of Little Big Horn**. Around this time, Chief Joseph attempted to lead his Nez Perce tribe to Canada; this mission failed and the Nez Perce were sent to Oklahoma. The Apache leader Geronimo was defeated in Arizona in 1887. At the **Battle of Wounded Knee**, the US army massacred 300, mostly women and children. Native Americans were doomed by their inferior weapons; by the destruction by whites of their food supply, the buffalo; and by railroads which made it easier for whites to encroach on their hunting grounds.

Solutions to the "Indian Problem"

The US government constructed several policies in an attempt to solve the so-called "**Indian Problem**." The **Dawes (Severalty) Act of 1887** asserted that Natives needed to be assimilated into American society; tribes were moved onto "allotments of severalty" (reservations), which they supposedly owned, although they had no control of the land. The **Indian Reorganization (Howard-Wheeler) Act of 1934** encouraged a return to tribal life, and offered Natives money for college. In 1953, with the so-called "**termination policy**," Natives became the responsibility of the states rather than the federal government. In 1970, the new strategy was "self-determination without termination": Natives were allowed to move where they choose, and were promised money (which they did not receive).

Era of Bonanzas

Between the years 1848 and 1858, the miners known as the "**forty-niners**" dug about $555 million out of the Western soil. In particular, the **Comstock Lode** of Virginia City, Nevada was famous for producing vast amounts of gold and silver. After buffalo were largely eradicated from the Great Plains, there was a "cattleman's bonanza," aided by the invention of barbed wire. The **Cattleman's Association** was a union of cattle dealers joined together to preserve the integrity of the industry, to stop cross-breeding, and to stop cattle thievery. This era marked the end of the open range, mainly because of horrible droughts and bad winters, range wars between the cowboys and sheep farmers, the railroads and barbed wire.

Homestead Act of 1862 and the Transcontinental Railroad

The US government tried many different ways to improve conditions for farmers in the West. Under the **Homestead Act of 1862**, farmers were sold 160 acres for $10, with the proviso that they had to improve the land within 5 years. Between the years 1865 and 1900, only one in six farms began this way. The **Timber Culture Act of 1873** gave more land to farmers, with the proviso that they had to plant some trees on that land.

One thing that helped to populate the West was the completion of the **Transcontinental Railroad** in 1869. The Union Pacific met the Central Pacific railway at Promontory Point, Utah. In 1889, the US government opened Oklahoma for settlement, and by 1893 it was completely settled.

Second Industrial Revolution

The Second Industrial Revolution was possible in the United States because of the abundance of raw materials and the laissez-faire economic policies of the government. In the space between the years 1860 and 1914, industry grew to about twelve times its original size. This rapid progress was made possible by the rapid growth of the **American railway system**. The railroads were subsidized by the federal government. Around this time, Samuel Morse developed his **telegraph code**, enabling almost instantaneous communication across vast distances. Jay Gould and James J. Hill were among those who made immense fortunes as railroad managers. Cornelius Vanderbilt and his son William were both railroad magnates with a reputation for ignoring the plight of their workers.

Review Video: <u>Second Industrial Revolution</u>
Visit mometrix.com/academy and enter code: 608455

Review Video: <u>Second Industrial Revolution: Standard Oil Company</u>
Visit mometrix.com/academy and enter code: 616068

Review Video: <u>Second Industrial Revolution: The American Railroad System</u>
Visit mometrix.com/academy and enter code: 843913

Industrial Era Scandals and Innovations

The infamous **Credit Mobilier scandal** occurred during Grant's presidency and involved the Union Pacific Railroad. A more egregious crime was perpetrated on the stockholders of the Erie Railroad; the owners were trying to avoid being bought out by Vanderbilt, and thus they printed up a huge amount of new stock, making it impossible for Vanderbilt to get a majority interest but also vastly diminishing the value of each share. During this era, the following **innovations** and inventors accelerated industry: sleeper cars (George Pullman); air brakes for trains (George Westinghouse); time zones; double tracking (so that two trains could run on the same line); and the standardization of the distance from one rail to another,

Competition and Disorder in the Industrial Era

The late eighteenth century was marked by intense **competition** between the railroads. Railroads offered secret illegal refunds to big customers and in areas where they had no competition, they charged exorbitant prices. After the 1870s, various states tried to tame the railroads; one such instance of this kind of regulation was the **Granger Laws**. Farmers often felt that they were charged more than others. In **Munn v. Illinois** (1877), the Supreme Court asserted that the state governments had the right to regulate the railroads. In Wabash, St. Louis, and **Pacific Railroad Co. v. Illinois** (1886), the Supreme Court reversed its former opinion and declared that only the federal government could regulate the railroads. Finally, with the **Interstate Commerce Act of 1887**, the federal government forbade discriminatory practices like refunds and price fixing; unfortunately, these laws were rarely enforced.

J.P. Morgan and Banker Control

The **Panic of 1893** was brought on by the collapse of the **Philadelphia and Reading Railroads**; soon after, 192 railroads failed. In a panic, railroad magnates turned to bankers, especially the "Railroad Doctor," **J.P. Morgan**. Morgan insisted that all of the business' records be opened to him. His usual strategy was to encourage old investors to reinvest, to sell more, "watered-down" stock, and to place either himself or one of his associates on the Board of Directors. In this way, Morgan was able to create a set of "interlocking directories," conglomerations of businesses in which he had an interest. He created many large companies this way, among them General Electric, Western Union, and Equitable.

Andrew Carnegie and Steel

The potential for making money in **steel** was made possible by the development of the **Bessemer process**, whereby iron ore was converted into wrought iron and then has its impurities removed with cold air. **Andrew Carnegie**, an immigrant from Scotland who rose to the top of the Pennsylvania Railroad, was one of the first to make his fortune in steel. He was not especially knowledgeable about steel, but he was the first manager to make a point of **vertical integration**: that is, control of every step of the production process. Carnegie bought out most of his competitors, until he was eventually bought out by J.P. Morgan. Carnegie and his fellows believed in a sort of "gospel of wealth," the idea that they had risen to the top through a process like natural selection. They also believed in using their money for the community.

> **Review Video:** Andrew Carnegie and the Steel Industry
> Visit mometrix.com/academy and enter code: 696753

John D. Rockefeller and the Trust

John D. Rockefeller came from a working-class background, but gradually rose to become the owner of the wildly profitable **Standard Oil company**. Rockefeller was known for spying on his competitors and intimidating his employees. In 1870, Standard allied itself with 40 other companies; when this alliance began, the group controlled 10% of the market, but by 1881 they controlled almost 95%. In 1882, Standard Oil created a **trust**: alliance members gave their stock to Standard in exchange for trust certificates. The federal government began to get suspicious of these powerful trusts, and in 1890 the **Sherman Anti-trust Act** was passed. This act forbade trusts, but it was worded so vaguely that it was ineffective. In the case of **US v. E.C. Knight Co.** (1895), the Supreme Court ruled that the Knight sugar refinery was not a monopoly because it didn't hurt interstate trade; businesses saw this ruling as a call to monopolize.

Laissez-Faire Conservatism and the Gospel of Wealth

The so-called "**Gilded Age**" of American history, which ran roughly from 1880 to 1900, only looked prosperous from a distance. Many at this time believed that wealth justified itself, and that God showed his favor in people by making them rich. Many business leaders did not trust politicians because they did not feel that they had had to fight their way to the top. Businessmen believed that the role of the government was to protect property and trade through tariffs. **William Graham Sumner** wrote the essay "What the Social Classes Owe Each Other," in which he declared that corporations shouldn't demand high tariff rates, but the government shouldn't respond to requests to clean up the slums. There was a general sense that the poor were responsible for their plight. Around this time, the popular imagination was inspired by the rags-to-riches fables of **Horatio Alger**.

Social Critics and Dissenters in the Gilded Age

In his book *Dynamic Sociology*, **Lester Frank Ward** railed against the Social Darwinism espoused by the upper class; he declared that humans were more than mere animals. In *Progress and Poverty*, **Henry George** asserted that poverty was the result of poor legislation rather than any inherent weakness in the poor. **Edward Bellamy** promoted socialism in his novel *Looking Back* (1888); in it, a man of the year 2000 describes how America was turned into a utopian society through the abolition of corporations. Also at this time, **Thorstein Veblen** exposed the phenomenon of "conspicuous consumption" in his *Theory of the Leisure Class*. All of these critics were disgusted by the hypocrisy of the **robber barons**; these magnates claimed to support laissez-faire government, yet they wanted high tariffs to protect their businesses.

American Labor in the Gilded Age

As the US emerged from the Civil War, one of the main economic problems was that most workers were **unskilled**. In general, working conditions were horrendous and wages were low. There was little homogeneity in the labor force, either, making it difficult for workers to switch jobs. **Immigrants** were usually willing to take more dangerous jobs than natives; during the 1880s, more than 5 million immigrants entered the US. In 1882, the **Chinese Exclusion Act** put a 10-year moratorium on Chinese immigration. In 1885, the **Foran Act** prohibited American business men from traveling to China to recruit workers. Both of these acts were open violations of the **Burlingame Treaty of 1868**, which had provided for open Chinese immigration.

> **Review Video:** The Gilded Age: An Overview
> Visit mometrix.com/academy and enter code: 684770
>
> **Review Video:** The Gilded Age: Chinese Immigration
> Visit mometrix.com/academy and enter code: 624166
>
> **Review Video:** The Gilded Age: Labor Strikes
> Visit mometrix.com/academy and enter code: 683116
>
> **Review Video:** The Gilded Age: Labor Unions
> Visit mometrix.com/academy and enter code: 749692

Labor Organizations After the Civil War

National Labor Union and Noble and Holy Orders of the Knights of Labor

At the end of the Civil War, only about 2% of all US workers were **unionized**; many believed joining a union was an admission that one would never move up. Over time, though, people began to realize that the consolidation of business interests (trusts) had to be met by a consolidation of labor. In 1866, the **National Labor Union** was founded by William H. Sylvis; this idealistic organization advocated an 8-hour work day but disbanded after backing the loser in the 1872 election. In 1869, Uriah Stephens founded the **Noble and Holy Orders of the Knights of Labor**; this group excluded doctors, lawyers, and bankers and supported the end of sexism; the 8-hour workday; paper money; income tax; and the prohibition of alcohol.

Haymarket Square and American Federation of Labor

In 1886, the **Knights of Labor** gathered in **Haymarket Square** in Chicago to protest an attack against another union. During the protest, a bomb was thrown and several people were killed; 7 members of the union were arrested, and some were executed. This incident linked labor unions with violence in the popular imagination. At the same time, less idealistic labor unions like the American Railway Union (led by Eugene V. Debs), the United Mineworkers, and the Molly McGuires were making great inroads in working communities. The **American Federation of Labor** was an alliance of many unions formed in 1881. This group sought a shorter workday, better working conditions, and workman's compensation: they were also not afraid to strike. The AFL frequently engaged in collective bargaining, in which a strike was threatened in order to bring management to the negotiation table.

Great Strike of 1877, the Homestead Strike, and the Pullman Strike

The Great Strike of 1877 occurred in West Virginia when state police and militiamen were sent to break up a railway strike and joined it instead. President Hayes sent in the army and at least 100 people were killed breaking up the strike. This debacle set a bad precedent for future strikes. In the **Homestead (PA) Strike** of July 1892, a group of soldiers called by Henry Clay Frick (temporarily in charge of one of Carnegie's steel mills) brutally broke up a strike. In 1894, a group of **Pullman railcar employees** began a strike, supported by the American Railway Union of Eugene V. Debs. All rail workers then went on strike out of sympathy for the Pullman workers. The rail owners got an injunction, claiming that the rail workers were interfering with interstate trade and therefore violating the **Sherman Anti-trust Act**. This did not end the strike, and thus President Grover Cleveland had to send in the army under the false premise that the strike was holding up the US mail.

Opposition to Organized Labor

The general public **opposed** labor unions because they disliked the idea of closed shops (those places in which one had to be a union member to work) and because they had a reputation for violence. Unions were also fiercely competitive with one another, and there was some animosity between the unions for skilled and unskilled workers. Unions were always at a disadvantage in their dealings with management, in part because management could hire lobbyists (to promote anti-union legislation in Washington) and lawyers, and could bribe politicians. Owners often had blacklists of union trouble-makers who would not be hired, and plenty of "yellow-dog" workers who had signed contracts pledging never to join a union. Owners often hired spies to obtain information among workers, and, in the event of strike, they could always hire "scabs" to cross the picket lines. It was not unheard of for managers to hire thugs to cause trouble among strikers and perpetuate the rowdy reputation of the unions.

Gilded Age

Characteristics

The period in American history between Reconstruction and the Progressive Era is commonly known as the **Gilded Age**. During this period, the US seemed to be simultaneously abandoning the ideals of the past and failing to anticipate the future; this was in large part due to the confusion of a horrendous Civil War and massive immigration, industrialization, and urbanization. During this period, many Americans sought refuge in **community organizations** like the Moose Lodge, the Elks Club, and the Masonic Lodge. The politicians of the Gilded Age tended to avoid the major issues of **social injustice and inequality**, instead focusing on minor issues like public v. parochial schools, and the blue laws (laws restricting commercial activity on Sunday).

> **Review Video: The Progressive Era**
> Visit mometrix.com/academy and enter code: 722394

Politics

Although the **Republicans** dominated the executive branch during the Gilded Age, Congress was evenly divided. The Republican party was composed mainly of people from the Northeast and Midwest. Blacks typically were Republicans (that is, when they were allowed into the political process). In general, the Republicans supported high tariffs and sound money. One of the main internal disputes in the Republican party was between the **stalwarts**, who supported the spoils system, and the **half-breeds**, who did not. As for the **Democrats**, they were largely based in the

South or in the big cities of the North. The Democrats and Republicans butted heads over ethnic, religious, and cultural issues, but they tended to avoid larger economic and social issues. Extremely talented individuals were more likely to go into business than politics during this era. Another trend of the Gilded Age was the domination of the president by Congress.

Hayes Presidency

<u>Highlights</u>

Foolishly, **Rutherford B. Hayes** made himself a lame-duck president by announcing soon after taking office that he would not seek a second term. Hayes' wife was nicknamed "Lemonade Lucy," because she would not allow any alcohol in the White House. Hayes tried to restore the power of the presidency after the debacle of Grant, but he was weakened by intense struggles over his Cabinet confirmations. One thing Hayes can be credited with is making a gallant attempt to destroy the **spoils system**. He replaced the Collector of the Customs House after discovering the corruption of that body, and he appointed Carl Schurz Secretary of the Interior on the basis of merit. In turn, Schurz established a merit system in his department, creating an entrance exam for potential employees.

<u>Lowpoints</u>

One of the failures of the Hayes administration was its handling of the **Great Rail Strike of 1877**. When over two-thirds of the rail lines were shut down by strikes, Hayes sent in federal troops, and there was considerable bloodshed. This set a bad precedent for how strikes would be handled in the future. Hayes vetoed an attempt by western labor unions to restrict Chinese immigration, saying that this would be a violation of the **Burlingame Treaty**. One of the main issues in the Hayes years was monetary policy. Farmers, who were often in debt, wanted a soft currency not backed by anything; they were willing to settle for a silver standard. In **Hepburn v. Griswold** (1869), the Supreme Court had ruled that there could not be paper money without a gold standard; in the **Legal Tender cases of 1871**, however, the Court reversed itself. The bickering over these conflicting rulings plagued the Hayes administration.

<u>Hayes vs. Greenbackers and the Silverites</u>

After the **Specie Resumption Act of 1875**, Hayes worked to minimize the effects of the oncoming "day of redemption," in which paper money could be exchanged for gold coins. He began a policy of contraction, wherein the government gradually took in paper money and issued gold, and he funded attempts to mine more gold. The **Greenbackers** were those who wanted Hayes to postpone the day of redemption; he did not, and it ultimately proved anticlimactic, as people assumed their paper money was "good as gold" and didn't bother to redeem it. Hayes also had to deal with the **Silverites**. In 1873, the government had enraged silver prospectors by announcing that it would no longer make coins out of silver. In answer to their fury, Hayes pushed through the **Bland-Allison Act**, which established that a minimum of $2 million of silver had to be purchased and coined by the government every month.

Election of 1880

In the election of 1880, the **Republican party** was beset by internal squabbling between the stalwarts and half-breeds over the issue of patronage. This led to a chaotic nominating convention in which a campaign manager, **James A. Garfield**, became the candidate. Garfield won a narrow victory over the Democrat Winfield Scott Hancock, a war hero with no political experience. Garfield was a charismatic figure whose administration began with a successful compromise among Republicans; unfortunately, he was shot and killed in 1881. Garfield was succeeded by his vice-president, **Chester A. Arthur**. The major event of his presidency was the **Civil Service Act of 1883**, which established a commission to create competitive examinations for potential government employees. Arthur also helped create the modern US navy.

Election of 1884

In 1884, the incumbent Arthur was passed over by his party in favor of Secretary of State James G. Blaine. This proved to be a bad move, as the **Democratic** candidate, **Grover Cleveland**, was able to win the support of conservative Republicans (Mugwumps) and claim a narrow victory. The highlights of the Cleveland administration include the further reform of civil service and the government's successful stand against ex-Union soldiers who were protesting for large pensions. Cleveland reluctantly signed the **Interstate Commerce Act**, and he was correct in predicting that it would not be enforced. Cleveland also spent a great deal of time on tariffs: he attempted to reduce the overall duty with the **Mongrel Tariff** and the **Mills Bill of 1888**, neither of which were very successful.

Election of 1888

In 1888, the Republican **Benjamin Harrison** narrowly upset the incumbent Cleveland, despite having less of the popular vote. Harrison did not accomplish much civil service reform, and spent a great deal of time managing insubordination in Congress. Harrison's Republican agenda promoted the **Federal Election Bill**, which was a response to the Mississippi Plan designed to protect the voting rights of freedmen. The **Silver Purchase Bill** was favored by the west, but lacked the votes to get through. In the **Compromise of 1890**, the Western Republicans got the silver purchase (Sherman Silver Purchase Act), Southern Democrats got the defeat of the Federal Election Bill, and the Northern Republicans got a higher tariff (McKinley Tariff of 1890). Harrison's administration became known for giving money away for virtually any reason: pensions were excessive; the silver purchase cost federal money; and all of the income tax taken during the Civil War was given back to the people.

Agricultural Problems During Populism

In the years following the Civil War, the US heartland suffered from an **overabundance** of wheat and rice; these surpluses, coupled with the advances in transportation and communication, drove prices down. Farmers were forced into high debt which they could never repay, leading to **deflation** and a scarcity of currency. Since many farmers didn't own the land that they worked, the banks often had to **foreclose** when farmers were unable to pay their debts. Farmers blamed their problems on a number of different factors. They blamed the railroads, which usually gave discount rates to bigger shippers. They blamed the banks, which loaned money to the rich but were unforgiving of farmers' economic plight. They also blamed the tax system, claiming that it was easy for businesses to hide their assets and impossible for farmers to do so. Additionally, they blamed the tariff, which discouraged other countries from buying US goods.

Early Farm Organization During Populism

The **Patron of Husbandry (Grange)** was founded in 1867 by Oliver Kelley to establish cooperatives, in which individuals bought goods directly from the whole-sale distributor. His group was also responsible for the **Granger Laws**, which attacked railroad and grain elevator interests. The Grange had basically disappeared by 1875. The **National Farmer's Alliance and Industrial Union** pursued a number of different initiatives: more national banks; cooperatives; a federal storage system for non-perishable items; more currency; free coinage of silver; reduction of tariffs; direct election of senators; an 8-hour workday; government control of railroads and telegraphs;

- 54 -

and one term for the president. This group's success led to the formation of the **Populist Party** in 1890. This party aimed to speak for the farmers and included all of the farmers' unions as well as some labor unions, the Greenbackers, and the Prohibitionists. The party suffered from internal divisions from its inception.

Election of 1892 and the Panic of 1893

Grover Cleveland (Dem) defeated Benjamin Harrison (Rep) in the election of 1892 primarily because of his financial conservatism, his promise to change the tariff and because the epidemic of strikes in 1892 had weakened Harrison. Then came the **Panic of 1893**, caused by labor troubles, overspeculation in the railroads, and an agricultural depression. First the Philadelphia and Reading Railroads collapsed, then the stock markets collapsed, then the banks folded, draining the gold reserves, then the other railroads folded, and finally the factories were forced to close. Cleveland believed that the cause of this Panic was the **Sherman Silver Purchase Act**, so he repealed it. This plan did absolutely nothing financially, and it split the Democratic party politically.

Panic of 1893 and Domestic Affairs Under Cleveland

After the Panic of 1893, a group known as the **Silverite school** declared that the economic problems could be solved if the US would begin coining silver again. Cleveland, however, ignored this advice, and elected to buy gold with the profits from the sale of government bonds. This strategy was somewhat successful. It was during the **Panic of 1893** that the suggestion to battle economic depression by employing people on public works was first made. One of Cleveland's major policy moves in his second term was the **Wilson-Gorman Tariff of 1894**. This lowered the tariff rate and established trade with Latin America. It also established a small income tax on wealthy individuals, though this income tax would be repealed in the **Supreme Court case Pollock v. Farmer's Loan and Trust** (1895). Cleveland's last term was diminished by ineffective enforcement of the **Sherman Anti-trust Act** and the **Interstate Commerce Act**.

Republican Ascendancy in the Election of 1896

The Republicans had been successful in the Congressional elections of 1894, and they nominated **William McKinley** for president in 1896. McKinley was in favor of high tariffs and the gold standard. He was opposed by William Jennings Bryan of the Democrats. McKinley had a wealth of political experience and money, and the Democrats were blamed by many for the economic depression under Cleveland: McKinley won fairly easily. This election marked a 36-year period of domination by the **Republicans**. It also spelled the end of the Populist party. Around this time, gold was found in the Yukon, lending credence to the Republican belief in the gold standard.

Imperialism

During the Period of Withdrawal (Civil War to 1880s)

In the period after the Civil War, the US for the most part withdrew from **foreign affairs**. The Secretaries of State in this period, however, were very aggressive: **Seward** interfered in Korean politics, tried to assert influence in the Caribbean, and famously purchased Alaska from Russia in 1867 for $7.2 million. **Hamilton Fish** tried and failed to annex Santo Domingo. Aside from these instances, though, the US kept its distance. For the most part, this was because it was preoccupied with its own problems. There was also a common belief that invading and colonizing other countries would be a violation of our own **Declaration of Independence**. Many were remembering Washington's farewell address, in which he advised the US to avoid military entanglements, and others were wary of violating the **Monroe Doctrine**.

During the New Manifest Destiny (1880s to 1920s)

In the 1880s, the US began to take a stronger interest in **foreign affairs**. This was in part due to humanitarian concern: the US felt it could improve the standard of living around the world. There was also, of course, an economic motive; manufacturers wanted to find a new source of raw materials, as well as a new market for their products. Missionaries began to travel abroad in this period, trying to convert foreigners to Christianity. There were also military reasons for the increased activity abroad; the US decided it would be a good idea to acquire naval bases in the Pacific and a group known as the **Jingoists** openly looked for a military conflict. Theodore Roosevelt and Henry Cabot Lodge were both Jingoists.

Bering Sea, Pan-American Union, and Samoan Islands Conflict

The "**Seal Battle**" was fought in the Bering Sea between British Canada and the US mainly over boundary lines. In 1893, the two sides met and established mutual boundaries between Alaska and Canada. In 1889, the first meeting of the **Pan-American Union** was held in Washington, DC. In 1878, the US had established a naval base at Pago Pago. Both the British and Germans demanded access to the base. In 1889, the US allowed both the British and Germans to jointly occupy the base. In 1899, the **Samoan islands** were divided up among the US and the European powers.

Conflict with Italy, Baltimore Incident, Boundary Disputes in South America, and Hawaii

Between the years 1889 and 1891, the US came into conflict with **Italy** after members of the **Sicilian Black Hand**, a terrorist group, were lynched without just cause in New Orleans. The US also sparred with Chile after 2 sailors from the *USS Baltimore* died during a bar fight in Valparaiso, Chile. At around this time, a boundary dispute erupted between **British Guiana** and **Venezuela** after gold was discovered in the vaguely-defined border region. Britain was ready to send troops into South America but the US dissuaded them from doing so, citing the Monroe Doctrine. Meanwhile, all throughout the nineteenth century the US had been closing in on a conquest of **Hawaii**. After New England missionaries stumbled upon the islands, the US had gotten the natives to sign trade treaties with various US companies. In the 1890s the US army, led by pineapple magnate Sanford Dole, ousted the native leadership. Hawaii was annexed by the US in 1898.

> **Review Video: Anti-Colonial Struggles: Central and South America**
> Visit mometrix.com/academy and enter code: 158300

Spanish-American War

Causes

The **Spanish-American War** centered around **Cuba**. There had already been several revolts against the Spanish leadership on that island, and the **Wilson-Gorman Tariff** had damaged the Cuban economy. In 1896, the Spanish sent General Valeriano Weyler to establish a reconcentration camp, where the dissenting Cubans could be weeded out. Many in the United States pushed the government to intervene in Cuba; businessmen were worried about their crops, Christians and humanitarians were worried about the Cuban people, and imperialists saw a good chance to seize the island. The two final causes of the war were the **DeLome letter**, in which the Spanish minister to the US insulted President McKinley, and the explosion of the *USS Maine* in Havana Harbor. Although the Spanish still claim to not have caused this explosion, the US nevertheless declared war on April 25, 1898.

<u>Overview</u>

The Spanish-American War only lasted between six and eight weeks before the US claimed victory. The first phase of it was fought in the Philippines, and the second in Cuba. In Cuba, the United States scored a crucial victory when a rag-tag group of soldiers known as the **Roughriders** (Theodore Roosevelt among them) took Kettle Hill and secured Santiago. Although the **Teller Amendment of 1898** had promised independence to Cuba after the war, the **Platt Amendment**, which was inserted into the Cuban Constitution in 1901, made Cuba a protectorate of the US. The US control of **Guantanamo Bay** dates back to this amendment. In 1934, Cuba received its independence. The Spanish-American War formally ended with the signing of the **Treaty of Paris** in 1898. The US received Guam, the Philippines, Puerto Rico, Cuba, and Wake Island. The US also paid the Spanish $20 million because Manila had supposedly surrendered after the end of the war, making it an invalid wartime concession.

Debate over the Philippines and the Filipino War

In the years 1898 and 1899, the question of what to do about the **Philippines** was hotly debated in the US. **Imperialists** (including Henry Cabot Lodge and Theodore Roosevelt), wanted to make the group of islands into a state, argued against **Anti-imperialists** (e.g., Andrew Carnegie, Mark Twain) who felt that the US would be drawn into Asian conflicts. Some politicians, like William Jennings Bryan, voted for the Treaty of Paris and the acquisition of the Philippines because they felt it would be a disaster that would discourage further imperialism. In 1899, the Filipino leader **Aguinaldo** led the people against US forces. This uprising was only crushed after much cruelty. Later, the **Tydings-McDuffie Act of 1934** promised independence to the Philippines within 10 years but they did not receive it until 1946. Some relevant Supreme Court rulings from this period were in the **Insular Cases of 1901**: the Court asserted that citizens of US territories do not have the same rights as citizens of the continental US.

Hampton Roads Peace Conference, Last Battles of Civil War, and Assassination of Lincoln

At the Hampton Roads Peace Conference in February of 1865, **Lincoln** and Secretary of State **Seward** met with the vice president of the CSA, **Alexander Stephens**. Lincoln made a stern offer: reunion of the states, emancipation of the slaves, and immediate disbanding of the Confederate army. The Confederates, however, were not yet ready to return to the Union. The Northern General U.S. Grant then led troops toward the CSA capital at Richmond. Finally, at **Appomattox** (VA) in April of 1865, Lee surrendered to Grant. Soon after, the Confederate President **Jefferson Davis** would be caught and jailed. Finally, on April 14, 1865, Lincoln was fatally wounded by two shots from the gun of **John Wilkes Booth** in Ford's Theater in Washington.

Lincoln's Reconstruction Plan

According to Lincoln, the relation between the North and the South after the completion of the Civil War would include "malice for none, charity for all." He imagined that the President would lead the **Reconstruction** effort, and, in 1863, he vowed that once 10% of the 1860 voters in a Southern state pledged loyalty to the Union, they could draft a new state constitution and receive "executive recognition." Lincoln was unsure whether blacks should be gradually emancipated or relocated, but he knew they should be free. As for his own **Republican party**, Lincoln asserted that it should become a national party, and that it should include freed blacks, who would receive the right to vote.

Congress' Reconstruction Plan

With the **Wade-Davis Bill of 1864**, Congress outlined their plan for the rehabilitation of the South after the Civil War. Unlike Lincoln, who had only asked for a 10% (of 1860 voters) loyalty nucleus, Congress wanted a majority before admitting Southern states back into the **Union**. Participants in the state constitutional conventions would be required to sign an "ironclad oath" pledging eternal loyalty to the Union. Ex-Confederate officials would not be allowed to vote or hold office. Slavery, of course, would be **abolished**. Finally, the Confederate debt would be repudiated, and those who loaned money to the Confederacy would be unable to get it back. Lincoln **vetoed** this bill, mainly because he wanted the abolition of slavery to be an amendment rather than a law.

Presidential Reconstruction Plan Under Andrew Johnson

Andrew Johnson, a Jacksonian Democrat from Tennessee, became president after the assassination of Lincoln. Though a Southerner, he believed the yeoman farmers of the South had been tricked into war by "cotton snobs." Johnson's plan for reconstruction called for **amnesty** to be granted to all ex-Confederates except for high-ranking officials and wealthy cotton planters, who would be allowed to apply for special pardons. Johnson also called for a **provisional Unionist governor** to be appointed in each Southern state; this leader would hold a constitutional convention at which it would be necessary to disavow secession; repudiate the CSA debt; and accept the 13th amendment. This plan was largely a failure, however, because it infringed on the powers of Congress, was seen as too lenient on the South, threatened the Republicans by giving too much power to Southern Democrats, and ignored freed blacks, who were repressed in the South by the so-called **Black Codes**.

Radical Republican Reconstruction Plan

By 1867, Johnson's Reconstruction plan had largely failed. His unwillingness to change drove many moderate congressmen to become radicals. Radical Republicans came up with their own Reconstruction plan. First, a "Joint Committee of 15" went South to explore the damage done by the war; while there, they discovered the "Black Codes" repressing freed slaves. With the **Civil Rights Act of 1866**, they provided basic rights for ex-slaves (not including the right to vote). The **14th amendment** then gave blacks citizenship, and said that state governments could not deny anyone life, liberty and property without due process. This amendment disqualified ex-Confederates from holding public office, and declared that states could lose representation if they infringed on the rights of blacks. With the **Congressional Reconstruction Act** (Military Reconstruction Act) of 1867, the South was divided into 5 districts and placed under martial law; Congress forced this bill through, and eventually all of the Southern states capitulated.

> **Review Video: Reconstruction Era**
> Visit mometrix.com/academy and enter code: 790561

Tenure of Office Act and the Supreme Court's Activity

The Tenure of Office Act of 1867 established that in order to fire any Cabinet member, the president had to get the approval of the Senate. Though basically unconstitutional, this act almost ended the presidency of Johnson when he tried to dismiss **Edwin Stanton**, his Secretary of War. Johnson was charged with a crime, **impeached** by the House of Representatives, and missed being impeached by the Senate by one vote. The Supreme Court, though generally quiet during this period, made a couple of significant rulings. In **ex parte Milligan** (1866), the Supreme Court asserted that it is unconstitutional for military rule to continue after regular courts have been reinstated. In **ex parte**

McCardle (1868), a similar case, the Supreme Court was actually too afraid of Congressional radicals to make a ruling.

Radical Republican Reconstruction Governments in the South

Carpetbaggers were those Northerners who, under the guise of reinvesting in the Southern economy, took advantage of the situation by acquiring positions in local governments and raising taxes. **Scalawags** were those white Republican Southerners who took similar economic advantage. During the rule of the Reconstruction governments, blacks were allowed to hold some public offices, though not if they were freed slaves; the black Senator **Hiram Revels** (MS) served in Jefferson Davis' old seat. Blacks had very few economic rights and had no land. **Thaddeus Stevens** declared that blacks should receive "40 acres and a mule," but nobody was willing to take this land from its present owners. **Sharecropping** became basically another form of slavery. In short, the Reconstruction governments were corrupt, spent too much and levied too many taxes, and took advantage of newly-freed slaves. Still, these governments established state constitutions, built roads and schools, and made education compulsory.

Ku Klux Klan and Amnesty Act of 1872

In the 1870s, Southern whites, as members of the Conservatives or Redeemers, began to regain control of the local governments; they sought to do away with "Negro rule." The **Ku Klux Klan** was founded in 1867 by former Confederate General Nathan Bedford Forrest and other ex-Confederates. Though founded as a social club, this group quickly got out of hand, causing the passage of the **Ku Klux Klan and Force Acts** (1870-1), unsuccessful attempts to subdue the Klan by allowing for black militias. The **Amnesty Act of 1872** extended the right to vote to many more ex-Confederates. Gradually, the North began to lose interest in the South for the following reasons: they were disgusted by the corrupt governments; they were frustrated by the persistent racism; and they had agreed to remain distant in exchange for a higher tariff.

Election of 1868 and the Grant Administration

After the Civil War, the US was consumed by **materialism**. The election of 1868 pitted **Ulysses S. Grant** (Republican) against Horatio Seymour (Democrat). Grant was a war hero, and Seymour spent much of the campaign defending himself from allegations that he aided the Confederacy. The Democrats proposed that states should decide for themselves the question of black suffrage, and they wanted to give amnesty to former Confederates. Republicans had much more success with their campaign, blaming the Democrats for the war (a strategy known as "waving the bloody shirt"), and Grant won handily. Grant's presidency would not be as easy as his campaign, however. He had no political experience and was unused to compromise. He frequently fought with his Cabinet, though Secretary of State Hamilton Fish was able to convince him to sign the **Treaty of Washington** (1871), in which Britain compensated the US for aiding the Confederate navy.

Graft and Corruption Under Grant

Credit Mobilier Scandal, Schuylar Colfax, and Fisk-Gould Scandal

The Grant administration was so corrupt that the president himself had to apologize. One of the most famous fiascos of the era was the **Credit Mobilier scandal**: the Union Pacific gave a contract to the Credit Mobilier after the federal government secretly loaned Credit Mobilier money for their bid. Then, Vice-president **Schuyler Colfax** was caught accepting a bribe in return for ceasing the investigation. In the **Fisk-Gould scandal**, Jim Fisk and Jay Gould convinced Grant to keep government gold out of the New York Stock Exchange, because they hoped to corner the market.

Grant became angry with the men and dumped $4 million worth of gold onto the market. September 24, 1869 is known as **Black Friday** on Wall Street; this was the day that Grant's gold flood caused the price of gold to drop so rapidly that the entire market crashed. Gould was able to survive this catastrophe; Fisk was not.

Tammany Hall, Congressional Salary Grab, and Whiskey Ring Scandal

William Marcy "Boss" Tweed was the political boss of New York City. He ran the **Tammany H**all political machine, a group that fixed elections by recruiting voters with food and jobs. Another instance of corruption under Grant was the **Congressional salary grab**: Congress voted to give themselves a 50% raise, set retroactively by two years. The public was outraged by this avarice, and so, though they kept the pay raise, Congress gave up the back pay. In the **Whiskey ring scandal**, some tax agents who were supposed to be taxing barrels of whiskey were found to have been accepting bribes; this scandal went up as high as Secretary of the Treasury Benjamin Bristow. When historians look at this period and try to figure out why there was so much corruption, they generally decide that it was a carryover from the brutality of the war, combined with the naiveté of the president.

Opposition to Graft and Corruption Under Grant

Thomas Nast was one of the first famous political cartoonists; he made his name satirizing corrupt politicians like Boss Tweed. Grant established the **Civil Service Commission** in 1871, an organization whose mission was to study corruption and make recommendations to the president. Grant paid little attention to this group, however, and it died a quiet death in 1875. During Grant's first term, a group of upper-class Republicans, calling themselves the **Mugwumps**, began to call for a civil service based only on merit. At the same time, the **Liberal Republicans**, another splinter group of the Republican party, spoke out against the graft in civil service, the use of paper money and the Republican Reconstruction policy. This group supported a lower tariff and better treatment for farmers.

Election of 1872 and Final Collapse of Grant

In the election of 1872, **Grant** won a second term (over Liberal Republican Horace Greeley) because of his enduring status as a war-hero, and because the worst scandals of his administration had yet to be exposed. Quickly, though, Grant's administration fell apart. Five Cabinet members would be found guilty of **corruption**. Then came the **Panic of 1873**. This was the result of three factors: the withdrawal of European investment (Europeans were funneling their money into the Franco-Prussian War); the stock market crash caused by the Fisk-Gould scandal; and the inflexibility of the banks caused by heavy investment in non-liquid assets. As a result of these factors, **Jay Cooke and Co.**, one of the largest banks in the US, collapsed, taking several other banks with it. 89 railroads soon went under, and then the iron and steel mills had no business. By 1875, half a million Americans were unemployed, and farmers were beginning to lose their land to foreclosure.

Solutions to the Panic of 1873

By 1873, **currency deflation** was a major problem in the US. There were a number of supporters of cheap money, and they encouraged the US government to issue $26 million in greenbacks to stimulate the economy; this plan failed. There was another group of hard-money advocates who suggested using a gold standard, so the government made a compromise called the **Specie Resumption Act of 1875**. This act increased the number of national banks in the South and West; allowed national banks to issue as many notes as they wanted (up to a $300 million limit); and named a "day of redemption," on which all greenbacks could be exchanged for gold coins. The day of redemption never came to pass, however, which seemed to be a victory for the cheap money supporters. Instead, it became evident that the promise of gold exchange caused the public to treat greenbacks as if they were "good as gold." By 1879, the economy was back on track and the Republicans had acquired the reputation as the party in favor of business.

Election of 1876 and National Self-Evaluation

The election of 1876, won by **Rutherford B. Hayes** (Republican) over Samuel J. Tilden (Democrat), coincided with the **US centennial**, and so people were compelled to consider the history of the country thus far. When Americans of 1876 looked back, they had some reason to be pleased: they had survived a Civil War intact and had witnessed the end of slavery. They also had developed a strong national government. On the other hand, many Americans were disillusioned at this time by the scandals of the Grant administration. There had also been violent and disheartening struggles between black militiamen and the Ku Klux Klan in the South. Finally, many in the country were still reeling from Custer's bloody defeat at the Battle of Little Big Horn.

CLEP Practice Test

1. Place the following events related to Spanish colonization in their proper order. Place the earliest event first.

> I. The Treaty of Tordesillas divides the New World between Spain and Portugal
> II. Pizarro invades the Incan empire
> III. Balboa explores Panama
> IV. Cortés conquers the Aztec Empire.

a. I, II, IV, III
b. III, IV, I, II
c. I, IV, III, II
d. IV, III, II, I
e. I, III, IV, II

2. All of the following were reasons for disagreement over the legitimacy of British taxation EXCEPT

a. a lack of colonial representation in Parliament.
b. different perceptions of a separation of powers between Parliament and colonial legislatures.
c. the changeability of the English constitution and the set-in-stone quality of colonial charters.
d. different interests of colonial merchants and British joint-stock companies.
e. a split over the legitimacy of the French and Indian War.

3. During the Second Constitutional Convention, the Connecticut plan was developed as a compromise to the plans of which two colonies?

    a. Pennsylvania and Virginia
    b. New Jersey and New York
    c. Georgia and South Carolina
    d. New Jersey and Virginia
    e. Massachusetts and Pennsylvania

4. In Ben Franklin's Join, or Die cartoon, which of the original thirteen states is not represented?

    a. Massachusetts
    b. Vermont
    c. Georgia
    d. Virginia
    e. New York

5. What is salutary neglect?

    a. High taxation levels on British colonies without representation in Parliament
    b. Establishment of independent colonial legislatures
    c. A laissez-faire attitude towards colonial government
    d. Colonial indifference to British taxation
    e. Relaxed enforcement of British colonial laws related to foreign trade

6. Which of the following best describes the role of women in the American Revolution?

    a. Because America was still a patriarchal society, women were considered weaker and needed to be protected from the war.
    b. Women helped directly on the battlefield and fought beside the men on a regular basis.
    c. Women played a wide variety of roles, including cooks, seamstresses, nurses, maids, spies, launderers, and even secret soldiers
    d. They were not permitted near the battle lines, or the army camps, but could send help in the form of clothing and food.
    e. They were required to remain at home in order to raise their children while the men were off fighting

7. Who would agree most with the aims of the Boston Tea Party?

    a. Quebecois Francophones
    b. Redcoats
    c. American Tories
    d. Yankee merchants
    e. Southern farmers

8. Which two crops dominated Southern agriculture in the early 1700s?

    a. Tobacco and Wheat
    b. Rice and Tobacco
    c. Cotton and Rice
    d. Corn and Rice
    e. Tobacco and Peaches

9. The French and Indian War was significant because it

    a. directly led to the collapse of the British empire in North America.
    b. prompted a change in the British view toward the colonies' role in the empire.
    c. renewed French hostility toward Great Britain.
    d. united the colonies against British policies.
    e. ended Spanish influence in the western hemisphere.

10. "As Europe is our market for trade, we ought to form no partial connection with any part of it. It is the true interest of America to steer clear of European contentions. Europe is too thickly planted with kingdoms to be long at peace, and whenever a war breaks out between England and any foreign power, the trade of America goes to ruin, because of her connection with Britain…"

The sentiment of this passage best echoes:

    a. Patrick Henry's "Give Me Liberty" speech
    b. The Federalist Papers
    c. Washington's Farewell Address
    d. The Articles of Confederation
    e. The Declaration of Independence

11. What is mercantilism?

    a. A policy of opposition to international trade.
    b. The belief in merchants as the primary economic engines.
    c. The belief that colonies exist for the economic benefit of their home nations.
    d. A tactic involving wide-range taxation of colonial goods.
    e. The belief that colonies ought to be economically independent.

12. The United States was among the first nations to experience a sharp decline in birthrate during the period of the early republic. Which of the following was **NOT** a reason for that decline?

    a. Men migrating beyond the Appalachian Mountains increased the number of never married women.
    b. Women married later in life and had fewer children
    c. Men and women chose to limit their families with birth control
    d. Christians sought to preserve the virtue of young women
    e. Deaths during the revolution meant that fewer men were available to start families

13. Why was the Dominion of New England unpopular among Americans?

  a. Because it allowed James II to have more power over the colonies
  b. Sir Edmund Andros proved to be an ineffective leader in times of crisis
  c. England merely merged the colonies for profit
  d. The merger angered French and Spanish traders
  e. It led to an economic panic

14. Massachusetts, Pennsylvania, and Maryland were all colonies founded partly

  a. due to abundant natural resources
  b. in order to trade with natives
  c. to take advantage of trade routes
  d. because of massive indebtedness
  e. as refuges for minority religions

15. Which of the following was not a group who had to sacrifice a core belief to allow passage of the constitution?

  a. Slave States
  b. Small States
  c. Anti-Federalists
  d. Federalists
  e. Abolitionists

16. Why was the battle of Saratoga the turning point of the revolutionary war?

  a. It gave the American forces access to much needed supplies and gunpowder stores.
  b. It raised morale in the American navy.
  c. It convinced France to provide direct monetary and military support to the Americans against the British.
  d. It forced the British to retreat to the sea.
  e. It allowed Britain to cut through the American defenses.

17. Which of the following treaties did not involve access to the Mississippi River?

  a. Treaty of Paris (1763)
  b. Treaty of Paris (1783)
  c. Jay's Treaty (1795)
  d. Pinckney's Treaty (1795)
  e. Adams-Onis Treaty (1819)

18. Where was America's first written constitution, The Fundamental Orders, drafted?

  a. Connecticut
  b. Rhode Island
  c. Virginia
  d. New York
  e. New Jersey

19. The Paxton Boys would agree most on which of the following?

a. Frustration with lack of government provided protection on the frontier.
b. Abolition of the slave trade.
c. Ideas on revolution and breaking away from Britain.
d. No taxation without representation.
e. Unarmed, non-violent protest against Native American attacks on frontier farms.

20. Which preacher delivered the sermon "Sinners in the Hands of an Angry God"?

a. George Whitefield
b. Joseph Smith
c. Charles Finney
d. William Miller
e. Jonathan Edwards

21. Which of the following occurred as a result of the Whiskey Rebellion?

a. George Washington proved his ability to deal with rebellious citizens in a decisive way
b. The rebels were easily able to defeat the militia sent by Washington, proving the weakness of the United States military
c. The state militia put down the rebellion by itself, showing that the federal government could not handle domestic affairs well
d. Because of his swift victory over the rebels, Washington showed that he was unwilling to listen to the problems of the people
e. Because the Whiskey Rebellion such a small affair, Washington did not believe any direct action was necessary

22. Which of the following was **NOT** one of the disadvantages faced by the American colonies in the lead up to the American Revolution?

a. Britain's population was more than four times that of the colonies
b. Britain had a thriving economy
c. Britain had better knowledge of the colonial terrain
d. America's army was poorly trained
e. America lacked a central government and a source of tax revenue

23. The Navigation Acts of the 1600s were intended to

a. increase the manufacturing capabilities in the colonies.
b. regulate shipping by requiring navigation instruments.
c. promote British mercantilism by regulating shipping from the colonies.
d. stem the flow of immigration to the colonies.
e. stop French trade with New England.

24. Which of the following happened as a result of the Kentucky and Virginia Resolutions?

a. The idea of nullification of unconstitutional laws was introduced.
b. Both states agreed that the constitution could be read loosely.
c. The notion of implied powers was introduced into the federal government.
d. The presidency gained more powers to tax the people.
e. The people wanted a stronger central government.

25. All of the following is true about Britain before George Grenville became prime minister EXCEPT

    a. British citizens paid more than 5 times the amount in taxes than the colonists did.
    b. Most people in England considered Americans foreigners.
    c. American colonists paid more than 5 times the amount of taxes than the British citizens did.
    d. Britain, inspired by victories in previous wars, wanted a larger empire.
    e. Britain was in great debt from previous wars.

26. In 1782 a manumission act was passed by the Virginia assembly to allow its citizens to do which of the following?

    a. Purchase slaves directly from Brazil
    b. Take runaway slaves as their own property with no need to return them to their owner
    c. Buy and sell slaves free of taxation
    d. Free their slaves without a direct act of the Virginia assembly
    e. Allow African Americans to vote in local elections

27. The Triangular Trade was

    a. trade between the colonies with raw materials from the south being exchanged for manufactured goods from the north
    b. largely concerned with the lumber trade
    c. a system of exchanging European products for American raw materials
    d. a system of exchanging slaves, raw material, and manufacture between the Americas and West Africa
    e. limited to a few small regions of New England

28. New Netherland was divided up into large tracts of land called

    a. plantations
    b. manors
    c. encomiendas
    d. patroonships
    e. fiefs

29. Primogeniture refers to

    a. all land being inherited by a landowner's youngest son
    b. all land being inherited by a landowner's eldest child
    c. all land being inherited by a landowner's eldest son
    d. all land being equally divided between a landowner's sons
    e. all land being equally divided between a landowner's children

30. Anti-federalists opposed the Constitution for which of the following reasons?

a. The proposed constitution did not protect individual rights sufficiently and they feared the tyranny of a powerful federal government
b. The government it described was viewed as weak and incapable of resisting the British military
c. The government it sought to create failed to address the weakness of the Articles of Confederation
d. The government it would create left too much power in the hands of the states
e. The Constitution did not provide enough specifics in dealing with foreign powers

31. Emanuel Leutze's famous painting shown above depicts which American founding father crossing the Delaware on the way to the Battle of Trenton.

a. Thomas Jefferson
b. John Adams
c. Patrick Henry
d. George Washington
e. Alexander Hamilton

32. Which political philosopher argued that government comes from the consent of the governed?

a. Jean-Jacques Rousseau
b. Montesquieu
c. John Locke
d. David Hume
e. Thomas Jefferson

33. Why was the effect of the Boston Massacre?

    a. It was used to increase American Patriotism in opposition to the British.
    b. It led to the implementation of the Townshend Acts.
    c. It increased support for Loyalism in the Colonies.
    d. It showed the ineffectiveness of the Boston Tea Party.
    e. It led to the Declaratory Act.

34. Which of the following was NOT a characteristic of New England life?

    a. Land inheritance divided among all sons.
    b. Small, closely connected communities.
    c. Increasingly smaller land holdings as a result of repeated divisions.
    d. Strong religious belief stemming from Puritan theology.
    e. Mobile and fluid class systems.

35. King Philip's War, Bacon's Rebellion, and Lord Dunmore's War all have what in common?

    a. conflict over corruption of colonial governments
    b. conflict over a desire for more political freedom from Britain
    c. conflict over a desire for lower taxes
    d. conflict with Native Americans
    e. conflict with the French

36. What was the main reason the colony of Georgia was established?

    a. To set up trading posts in order to trade with Spanish Florida
    b. To have a place for debtors to begin a new life and eliminate their debt
    c. To open new ports for the Middle Passage
    d. To expand tobacco and rice production
    e. To alleviate overpopulation in the other colonies

37. "...our desire is not to offend one of his little ones, in whatsoever form, name or title he appears in, whether Presbyterian, Independent, Baptist, or Quaker. Therefore if any of these said persons come in love unto us, we cannot in conscience lay violent hands upon them, but give them free egresse and regresse unto our Town, and houses, as God shall persuade our consciences, for we are bounde by the law of God and man to doe good unto all men and evil to noe man."

The above quote is most consistent with the thoughts expressed in which of the following:

    a. the Olive Branch Petition
    b. the Federalist Papers
    c. the Fifth Amendment
    d. the First Amendment
    e. the Proclamation of 1763

38. Which monarch granted charters to Connecticut and Rhode Island?

    a. James I
    b. Charles II
    c. Charles I
    d. Elizabeth I
    e. William of Orange

39. Roger Williams, the founder of Rhode Island, is best known for

   a. his strong belief in the separation of church and state and freedom of conscience in religion.
   b. his opposition to slavery
   c. supporting universal white male suffrage for the colonies
   d. favoring a return to Anglican Church dominance in all British colonies
   e. his opposition to the conversion of Native American groups to Christianity

40. The Articles of Confederation did all of the following EXCEPT

   a. brought the states together in a "league of friendship."
   b. created a clear executive branch for the national government.
   c. allowed for the federal government to make treaties.
   d. created a postal service.
   e. allowed the federal government to declare war on other nations.

41. One criticism of George Washington's handling of the Whiskey Rebellion was that

   a. it was ineffective and failed to put down the rebellion.
   b. it was too heavy-handed and unwarranted.
   c. it caused too much bloodshed.
   d. it failed to effectively protect tax collectors.
   e. it hurt the national economy by lowering taxes.

42. Which of the following was a major focus of Hamilton's plan for the United States?

   a. Improve the economic status of the lower class.
   b. Improve public credit and make America an industrial world power.
   c. Dismantle the national debt and place the burden on the states.
   d. Create a strong economy based on agriculture.
   e. Improve relations with France rather than with England.

43. Place the following events that led to the American Revolution in their proper order. Place the earliest event first.

   I. Treaty of Paris (1763)
   II. Boston Massacre
   III. Siege of Fort Necessity
   IV. Sugar Act

   a. III, I, IV, II
   b. I, III, II, IV
   c. III, I, II, IV
   d. I, III, IV, II
   e. III, IV, II, I

44. Which region did Francisco Coronado explore?

   a. The North American Southeast
   b. Central America
   c. The North American Southwest
   d. Florida
   e. The Caribbean

45. When France allied with the American revolutionaries in 1778, it hoped that its role in the rebellion would allow it to seize British sources of which commodity in the New World?

    a. Sugar
    b. Tobacco
    c. Lumber
    d. Fur
    e. Gunpowder

46. Which of the following best describes the Enlightenment's effect on the drafting of the United States Constitution?

    a. The Enlightenment's focus on self-reliance inspired the Founding Fathers to emphasize remaining out of foreign conflicts
    b. The Enlightenment inspired the Founding Fathers to value individual liberty above all
    c. It had little to no impact on the writing of the Constitution
    d. The Enlightenment's focus on tolerance inspired the Founding Fathers to extend liberties to women and non-Whites
    e. The Enlightenment's focus on reason inspired the Founding Fathers to pursue a government that put power in the hands of the well educated

47. Which of the following best describes religious belief in the various colonies during the Colonial Era?

    a. divisive and institutional
    b. monolithic and totalitarian
    c. tolerant and peaceful
    d. unified and intolerant
    e. diverse and sectarian

48. The Necessary and Proper Clause of the Constitution is also called

    a. the implied clause and grants the Supreme Court judicial review.
    b. the elastic clause and grants Congress implied powers.
    c. the writ of mandamus and grants states rights under the 10th amendment.
    d. the supremacy clause and grants the executive branch the right to veto legislation.
    e. the habeas corpus clause and grants police the right to imprison people with probable cause.

49. Which of the following best describes the American people's attitude toward the French Revolution?

    a. Overwhelming support of it in all its facets
    b. Complete opposition to the revolutionaries, and sympathy for the monarchy and nobility
    c. Generally favoring the cause of liberty, but disagreeing with some of the more violent actions of the revolution.
    d. Neutral, with no preference to either side because of a desire to trade with whichever side won
    e. Generally sided with the monarchy because of France's alliance with the United States during the American Revolution

50. George Washington's government requested the removal of Edmond Charles Genêt as French Ambassador to the U.S. because

> a. he attempted to compromise American neutrality in the conflict between France and Britain.
> b. he was friendly to the overthrown government of Louis XVI.
> c. he was convicted of bribery in an American court.
> d. Thomas Jefferson advocated cutting ties with France.
> e. Washington was unhappy with French attempts to borrow money from the United States.

51. The Northwest Ordinances of the 1780s were notable for which of the following reasons

> a. They brought Oregon and surrounding territories into the Union
> b. They helped decide the question of slavery in new territories
> c. They doubled the available land for U.S. westward migration
> d. They continued the American practice of removing Native Americans from their territory through armed conflict
> e. They were the most significant thing to come out of the largely ineffectual Congress under the Articles of Confederation

52. Which of the following was both a signer of the Constitution yet accused of being a British Loyalist?

> a. John Dickinson
> b. Samuel Adams
> c. George Washington
> d. Ben Franklin
> e. Patrick Henry

53. Which best explains the significance of the Stamp Act?

> a. It led to the Boston Tea Party.
> b. It was the first English law designed to generate revenue from the colonies.
> c. It eliminated forgery in the colonies.
> d. It prompted the formation of the First Continental Congress.
> e. It caused the creation of the Committees of Correspondence.

54. Which of the following is true about the Middle Passage?

> a. It was the section of the triangular trade route in which rum was shipped to Africa for slaves
> b. It was a path used by settlers traveling to the frontier in the West
> c. It was the portion of the triangular trade route where slaves were brought from Africa to the Americas
> d. It was a trade route between the British colonies and French Louisiana
> e. It was a section of the triangular trade route where sugar was purchased in the Caribbean and transported to American ports in order to make rum

55. What was one of the biggest changes to come out of the First Great Awakening?

a. A strengthening of traditional beliefs and practices in the Congregational and Anglican churches throughout the colonies.
b. Growth of new denominations, especially Baptists and Methodists.
c. People supporting the revival because it strengthened community stability.
d. A call for the end of slavery as many African Americans converted to Christianity and were now spiritual "brothers".
e. Democracy was suppressed as new preachers and denominations required obedience from the faithful.

56. Which of the following is true regarding the XYZ Affair?

a. It increased tensions between Great Britain and the U.S. due to American friendliness with France.
b. It was a sign of American-French cooperation even after the French Revolution.
c. It fueled anger against France and lead to the undeclared "Quasi" war
d. It led to the 1800 victory of Thomas Jefferson following a spike in pro-British sentiment.
e. It signaled the end of American isolationism.

57. Which of the following was an effect of the Intolerable Acts?

a. Closure of the port of New York until reparations were paid.
b. Extension of Quebec's southern border.
c. Exorbitant taxes imposed on the colonies to recoup British military debt.
d. Increased unity between the colonies and direct support for the citizens of Massachusetts.
e. Creation of the Sons of Liberty to respond to British tyranny.

58. Benjamin Banneker was primarily known for his work in astronomy and

a. writing an almanac
b. foreign trade
c. city planning
d. being a poet
e. banking

59. Which of the following is NOT a reason Jamestown struggled during its first few years?

a. Its location adjacent to swamps and marshes led to disease
b. Somewhat hostile relationships with the Native Americans living in the region
c. Harsh winters and a difficult climate
d. The land was unfit for farming
e. The colonists chose to search for gold rather than farm

60. According to modern theories, how did the first humans most likely get to the Americas?

a. They crossed a land bridge connecting Alaska and Siberia.
b. They sailed from Asia to America.
c. They sailed from Spain to South America.
d. Humans originated in South America and spread upwards.
e. They sailed from England to Northern America.

61. During the election of 1848 Lewis Cass, the most vocal proponent of popular sovereignty, lost the election to Zachary Taylor. Members of which of the following pairs of groups would have been most likely to support Taylor?

    a. Anti-masons and Whigs
    b. Anti-masons and Free-soilers
    c. Free Soilers and Whigs
    d. Free Soilers and Locofocos
    e. Locofocos and Whigs

62. The editorial cartoon from 1812, pictured above, was drawn to ridicule what type of policy in Massachusetts?

    a. Drawing of electoral districts for political advantage
    b. Imposing high tariffs on imports to protect local producers
    c. Allowing the establishment of an official religion for local counties
    d. Oppressively taxing the local counties to repay war debt
    e. Sectioning areas of land into distinct areas that allow or disallow slavery

63. In the Supreme Court decisions *Marbury v. Madison*, *McCulloch v. Maryland*, and *Gibbons v. Ogden*, John Marshall and the Supreme Court ruled in favor of

    a. the primacy of state power over federal power
    b. the primacy of federal power over state power
    c. the right of the federal government to regulate interstate commerce
    d. the right of the Supreme Court to review the decisions of lower courts
    e. the right of the federal government to establish a national bank

64. For what reason did Chicago replace Cincinnati as the nation's leading supplier of pork during the Civil War?

    a. The demand for pork products significantly decreased due to the war
    b. Chicago's use of advanced technological methods made it efficient
    c. Cincinnati's ability to export via the Mississippi River was limited
    d. Chicago had a larger number of immigrant workers who could staff growing factories
    e. Cincinnati's close proximity to Kentucky made it a target for southern raiders

65. To which of the following groups would the Know-Nothing Party have most appealed?

    a. Southern farmers
    b. Catholics
    c. Immigrant factory workers
    d. Protestant artisans
    e. African-Americans

66. Which of the following is NOT a reason why people were upset with John Tyler's succession to the Presidency?

    a. He was a former Democrat succeeding a recently-elected Whig
    b. He was in conflict with the Whig-controlled Congress
    c. Americans were concerned over his lack of moral discipline
    d. He had a tendency to frustrate Democrats over policy disagreements
    e. Americans doubted the legitimacy of his presidency after the death of W.H. Harrison.

67. Place the following events that relate to the annexation of Texas in the correct chronological order with the earliest first.

    I. Texas declares independence from Mexico
    II. America defeats Mexico in the Mexican-American War
    III. Texas is annexed by the U.S.
    IV. Mexico wins independence from Spain

    a. I, II, III, IV
    b. III, II, IV, I
    c. II III, IV, I
    d. IV, I, II, III
    e. IV, I, III, II

68. Why was the Erie Canal significant?

    a. It dramatically lessened the time and the cost of moving goods from inland markets to the harbor in New York.
    b. It helped connect Canadian manufacturing to American markets.
    c. Its inefficiency helped the nascent railroad industry.
    d. It was an engineering marvel
    e. It promoted the growth of New Orleans as an economic hub linking the nation, North to South.

69. Place the following events that led up to the Civil War in the correct chronological order with the earliest first.

    I. The Wilmot Proviso is first proposed
    II. Nat Turner's rebellion
    III. The election of Abraham Lincoln as President
    IV. The Missouri Compromise is passed

    a. IV, II, I, III
    b. I, II, III, IV
    c. II, IV, I, III
    d. II, IV, III, I
    e. IV, II, III, I

70. Which of the following best explains why the Democratic Party was split during the 1860 election?

    a. Conflict over whether the National Convention should be held in Charleston or Baltimore

    b. Democratic nominee, Stephen Douglas, advocated for high tariffs which would be detrimental to Southern cotton exports

    c. Northern and Southern Democrats were split on whether a transcontinental railroad should run through the North or the South

    d. Democratic nominee, Stephen Douglas, was considered a moderate on the slavery issue due to his embrace of popular sovereignty and rejection of the *Dred Scott* ruling

    e. Southern Democrats rejected Douglas because he was a Northerner

71. Which of the following states presently includes land area that was NOT ceded by Spain to the United States during the 19th century?

    a. Arizona

    b. Louisiana

    c. Colorado

    d. California

    e. Missouri

72. Which of the following regions was NOT a significant source of immigrants to the United States from 1830-1860?

    a. Ireland

    b. Great Britain

    c. Eastern Europe

    d. Central Europe including the lands that would become Germany

    e. France

73. In an 1818 treaty, the United States and Great Britain set the border between Canada and the U.S. at which of the following?

    a. 36° 30'

    b. 54° 40'

    c. 45°

    d. 39° 43'

    e. 49°

74. Which of the following was TRUE about the raid of the arsenal at Harpers Ferry?

    a. John Brown intended to capture the arsenal and use his position to bargain for the admission of Kansas as a free state.

    b. Northerners initially approved of John Brown's actions.

    c. John Brown intended to use the weapons seized to arm a slave revolt

    d. John Brown hoped that the raid would provoke a war between the North and South

    e. John Brown hoped to sell the weapons to buy the freedom of slaves

75. Which of the following had the greatest impact on the reform movements (like abolition, female suffrage, and temperance) that blossomed during the 19th century?

a. The Emancipation Proclamation
b. The Louisiana Purchase
c. The American Renaissance
d. The Second Great Awakening
e. The Enlightenment

76. Along with Missouri, the Compromise of 1820 allowed which state into the Union?

a. Arkansas
b. Kansas
c. Michigan
d. Maine
e. Alabama

77. The American painters known as the Hudson River School primarily focused on what theme?

a. American ingenuity depicted on large murals like *Detroit Industry*
b. Nature inspired scenes like *Kindred Spirits*
c. Rural scenes depicting authentic people like *American Gothic*
d. Historical Scenes like *Washington Crossing the Delaware*
e. Scenes depicting the new personal realities of urban areas like *Nighthawks*

78. Who is the author of the passage below based upon the impressions of its author in 1831.

In no country has such constant care been taken as in America to trace two clearly distinct lines of action for the two sexes and to make them keep pace one with the other, but in two pathways that are always different. American women never manage the outward concerns of the family or conduct a business or take a part in political life; nor are they, on the other hand, ever compelled to perform the rough labor of the fields or to make any of those laborious efforts which demand the exertion of physical strength. No families are so poor as to form an exception to this rule. If, on the one hand, an American woman cannot escape from the quiet circle of domestic employments, she is never forced, on the other, to go beyond it.

a. Elizabeth Cady Stanton
b. Frederick Douglas
c. Alexis de Tocqueville
d. Clara Barton
e. Lucretia Mott

79. Eli Whitney is remembered for his advocacy for which industrial innovation?

    a. Assembly Line
    b. Putting Out System
    c. Crop Rotation
    d. Eight-Hour work day
    e. Interchangeable parts

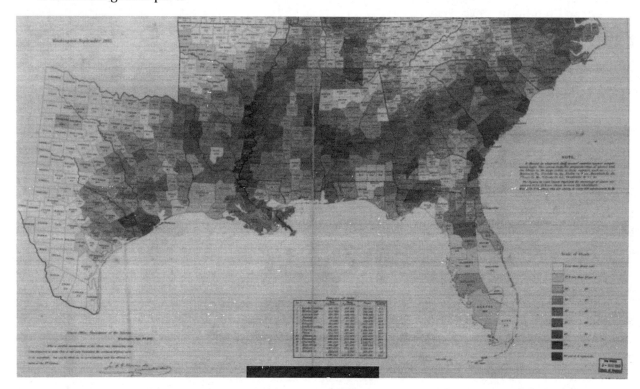

80. The 1861 map above, which shows the slave population of the Southern United States in 1860 by county, was created by the U.S. Coast Guard. (The higher the slave population the darker the color.) The map probably supports which inference below?

    a. Strongest support for Abraham Lincoln during the 1860 election
    b. The highest cotton producing counties
    c. The highest concentration of African American churches by county
    d. The highest tobacco producing counties
    e. The highest concentration of factories by county

81. All of the following are reasons American went to War against Britain in 1812 EXCEPT:

    a. An economic downturn caused by the Embargo Act led people to blame Britain
    b. American sailors were pressed into service by the British Navy
    c. Newer members of Congress especially from the South and West wanted war with Britain
    d. Americans had a desire to incorporate Canada into the U.S.
    e. The British seized Washington D.C. and burned the White House

82. Which of these is NOT associated with the Era of Good Feelings?

   a. The disintegration of the Federalist Party
   b. The continuation of the "Virginia Dynasty"
   c. The end of the first party system
   d. The movement towards the abolition of slavery
   e. The presidency of James Monroe

83. The gag rule was used to

   a. Determine whether or not to attack an African American freedman by the KKK
   b. Prevent popular sovereignty from deciding an issue in a given state
   c. Limiting African American slaves from having access to education so that they would not become literate
   d. Prohibiting debate over an issue in Congress
   e. Prohibiting female membership in reform movements

84. Which of the following best describes the 49'ers, the group who took part in the California Gold Rush before the Civil War?

   a. Business owners who usually left California no richer or poorer than before
   b. Young men who took on enormous debt to move West with most failing to strike it rich
   c. Former soldiers for hire with mining experience who became wealthy overnight
   d. Migrant workers moving to California in search of jobs and finding gold instead
   e. Wealthy business owners who jump-started California's economy through gold prospecting

85. Which plan for reconstruction called for full political and economic equality for freed slaves?

   a. Abraham Lincoln's plan
   b. Andrew Johnson's plan
   c. Henry Clay's plan
   d. Congressional plan controlled by the Republicans
   e. Democratic party's plan

86. Which of the following statements is consistent with the 1854 Ostend Manifesto?

   a. The United States would be justified in taking Cuba by force if Spain didn't sell it.
   b. Slavery should not be extended beyond its current boundaries.
   c. It was inevitable that the United States would control the entire North American continent.
   d. The United States ought to advocate free trade throughout the world and limit tariffs.
   e. Voting rights should be extended to immigrants and women.

87. The Louisiana Purchase and the Gadsden Purchase were similar in that

   a. They were both negotiated despite debate over whether the president was constitutionally allowed to do so.
   b. They were both meant to facilitate the construction of significant land-based infrastructure (like railroads).
   c. They both provided the United States access to economically important waterways.
   d. They both doubled the land area of the United States.
   e. They were both negotiated several years after the conclusion of hostilities with the country from which the land was purchased.

88. Which of the following was true of the American System?

  a. It encouraged the country to become economically self-sufficient
  b. It established a tariff for the sole purpose of raising revenue
  c. It prioritized the implementation of the telegraph
  d. It decreased defense spending to finance infrastructure projects
  e. It precluded the establishment of a national bank

89. Horace Mann played a major role in which reform movement?

  a. Prison reform
  b. Temperance movement
  c. Abolition
  d. Ending Sunday mail delivery
  e. Education reform

90. These lines are from the opening section of "When Lilacs Last in the Dooryard Bloom'd", an elegy by Walt Whitman.

  When lilacs last in the dooryard bloom'd,

  And the great star early droop'd in the western sky in the night,

  I mourn'd, and yet shall mourn with ever-returning spring.

  Ever-returning spring, trinity sure to me you bring,

  Lilac blooming perennial and drooping star in the west,

  And thought of him I love.

The poem was written in response to

  a. the end of the civil war following the surrender at Appomattox
  b. the end of slavery following the passage of the 13th amendment
  c. the death of Abraham Lincoln after he was assassinated at Ford's theater
  d. the secession of the southern states and the beginning of the Civil War
  e. the deaths of more than 22,000 Americans in a single day during the Battle of Antietam

91. The Free Soil Party was formed in the West because of

  a. overly high prices for Western lands
  b. concerns over slave labor undercutting farmers' revenues.
  c. moral opposition to slavery
  d. the Dred Scott case ending the Missouri Compromise
  e. fear of Mexican counterattack after the Texan annexation

92. Who wrote "The Star-Spangled Banner"?

  a. Henry Wadsworth Longfellow
  b. Walt Whitman
  c. Ralph Waldo Emerson
  d. Francis Scott Key
  e. Edgar Allen Poe

93. Which of the following was the cause of the Panic of 1837?

   a. The threat of war with Mexico because American Citizens were helping the revolution in Texas
   b. The surge in disease from new immigrants entering the U.S.
   c. Greatly reduced monetary reserves in Banks, higher interest rates, less lending, economic policies in the U.S. and abroad that led to steep deflation.
   d. Massive drought and wildfires in Western territories ravaging farms
   e. Native American uprisings against white frontier settlements

94. Why was the Waltham-Lowell System significant?

   a. It created a system of formal schooling for boys.
   b. It allowed African American freedmen to enter manufacturing in the north.
   c. It provided support for yeoman farmers in times of bad harvest.
   d. It allowed for more efficient harvesting of rice in South Carolina.
   e. It allowed northern women to take industrial jobs in textile mills.

95. During the nineteenth century, the Southern economy switched from primarily growing

   a. indigo to growing tobacco
   b. tobacco to growing cotton
   c. wheat to growing cotton
   d. cotton to growing coffee
   e. indigo to growing rice

96. Which of the following best explains the purpose of the Tariff of 1816?

   a. It was a protective tariff to help New England compete with imported French goods.
   b. It was designed to help decrease the large amount of national debt.
   c. It was a tax meant to punish Europeans nations like Britain and France for capturing neutral American merchant ships.
   d. It was a tariff intended to protect American manufacturers from cheaper British goods.
   e. It was intended to increase the cost of imported items that southerners needed to punish them for slavery.

97. Which of these was NOT a reason that the administration of John Quincy Adams was unpopular?

   a. His advocacy of federal funding for infrastructure improvements (i.e. roads, canals, etc.)
   b. His support for the "spoils system"
   c. His opposition to Cherokee eviction from Georgia
   d. Being elected president through the "corrupt bargain"
   e. His irritable and reserved personality

98. The passage below is taken from a speech given in the U.S. Senate on March 7, 1850 by Massachusetts Senator Daniel Webster. With his speech, the senator was advocating for which of the following positions?

> "Secession! Peaceable secession! Sir, your eyes and mine are never destined to see that miracle. The dismemberment of this vast country without convulsion! The breaking up of the fountains of the great deep without ruffling the surface! Who is so foolish, I beg every body's pardon, as to expect to see any such thing? Sir, he who sees these States, now revolving in harmony around a common centre, and expects to see them quit their places and fly off without convulsion, may look the next hour to see heavenly bodies rush from their spheres, and jostle against each other in the realms of space, without causing the wreck of the universe."

a. The abolition of slavery in Washington, D.C.
b. The admission of California as a free state in which slavery was forbidden
c. A strengthened fugitive slave law
d. A compromise that might help avoid violence over the issue of slavery
e. Support for the southerners who were upset over President Taylor's objections to the expansion of slavery into the western territories.

99. Andrew Jackson's victory in 1828 was most likely due to

a. his status as a wealthy, upper class, landed gentleman
b. the expansion of voting rights beyond large landowners and Jackson's status as a common man
c. his reputation for winning arguments and never backing down from a fight
d. his promise to reward his supporters through the use of the spoils system
e. being willing to comprise and work with Congress since the election had to be decided in the House of Representatives

100. Sharecropping was the system that emerged following the Civil War through which

a. Freed slaves were paid wages to work land for former slave-owners
b. Freed slaves pooled money to buy land to farm
c. Southern farmers worked with freed slaves for mutual profit
d. Pioneer Families in the West divided available farm land
e. Raw cotton was refined

101. Which of these groups most opposed the Second Bank of the United States?

a. Western farmers
b. Merchants
c. Eastern aristocrats
d. Federal Government employees
e. Legal scholars

102. The putting-out system refers to

a. United States' attempts to create a colonial empire
b. Organized settlement of pioneer families in the West
c. Production by individual families of finished goods
d. Rehabilitation of criminals so they could return to society
e. The freeing of slave children born in the US at the age of 18

103. Which of the following contributed most directly to tensions over slavery?

  a. The Trail of Tears
  b. Universal white male suffrage
  c. Demise of the National Bank
  d. The debate over the annexation of Texas
  e. The Panic of 1837

104. Which of the following best explains why the 1860 election was influential on future elections?

  a. It marked the first time that a presidential candidate actively campaigned for himself
  b. It cemented Republican electoral dominance in all regions of the country
  c. It was the first election to make use of modern campaign structures and tactics
  d. It was the first election in which the states of Kansas and Nebraska could vote
  e. It signified the final extinction of the Whig Party

105. Which of the following statements about economic policy in the election of 1840 is accurate?

  a. The Whigs supported reduced government spending.
  b. The Democrats supported Federal funding for infrastructure improvements.
  c. The Democrats were opposed to the power of the big banks.
  d. The Federalists supported the National Bank.
  e. The Democrats favored industrial interests over farmers.

106. Which document below best describes the primary reasons for the outbreak of the Civil War?

  a. The Emancipation Proclamation
  b. Lincoln's House Divided speech
  c. South Carolina Exposition and Protest
  d. The Tenth Amendment
  e. The Wilmot Proviso

107. The Underground Railroad was

  a. a rudimentary subway system in New York city
  b. a smuggling route for contraband slaves from Cuba
  c. a system of railroads unknown to the Confederacy which allowed the Union to resupply their troops more easily
  d. a system of people and homes used by southern slaves to escape to the North
  e. what replaced the pony express once the transcontinental railroad was completed

108. During the Civil war both the Northern States and the Southern States implemented requirements for compulsory military service. How did the two requirements differ?

  a. The northern law mostly affected the rich while the southern law targeted the poor.
  b. Avoiding military service required money in the North and owning slaves in the South
  c. The southern law sought to preserve farm productivity while the northern law sought to maintain factory productivity.
  d. The Northern draft had no possibility of exemption while the Southern draft allowed exemption to the owners of slaves.
  e. The Southern draft had no possibility of exemption while the Northern draft allowed exemption for money.

109. Which of the following would best exemplify sectionalism in the United States during the first half of the 19th century?

a. A northerner advocating for the division of slave and free states created in the Missouri Compromise
b. A senator from Kentucky asking for increased Federal government spending on infrastructure projects like canals and roads
c. A southerner speaking out against slavery
d. A factory worker from Massachusetts demanding lower tariffs
e. A senator from Virginia agreeing to the admission of California without conditions

110. The founder of the Utopian town New Harmony, Indiana would most likely agree with which of the following claims?

a. The church is central to religion.
b. Private ownership of property and capital is required for a healthy economy.
c. Men are superior to women in strength and intelligence.
d. Worker rights for collective bargaining, decent wages, an eight-hour work day are important.
e. Communal, democratic decisions are inefficient and lead to the tyranny of the majority.

111. What belief of the Second Great Awakening encouraged Christian participation in reform movements of the 19th century?

a. Predestination
b. God as triune
c. Equality of men and women
d. Free will to determine salvation
e. The importance of sacraments

112. Which of the following was NOT significant in determining the outcome of the 1844 election?

a. Manifest Destiny
b. The Liberty Party running an independent candidate
c. The annexation of Texas
d. Religious liberty
e. Slavery and abolition

113. Senators who voted in favor of impeaching Andrew Johnson likely did so because

a. he violated the Tenure of Office Act
b. he was disliked by the radical Republicans trying to enforce their form of Reconstruction
c. he was discovered to have secret Confederate sympathies
d. he refused to appoint Republican Supreme Court justices
e. he refused to endorse the fourteenth amendment

114. Which of the following was agreed upon in the Treaty of Ghent?

a. British acquired multiple territories previously held by the U.S.
b. Britain surrendered all of its North American holdings to the U.S.
c. All American borders were restored to their pre-war locations.
d. The United States and Britain agreed to form an anti-French coalition in North America.
e. The United States and France agreed to form an anti-British coalition in North America.

- 84 -

115. Which of the following statements best describes the Monroe Doctrine?

    a. It sought to protect the Western Frontier from Spanish incursion.
    b. It attempted to prevent European powers from interfering in the New World.
    c. It aimed to Increase trade between the United States and Europe.
    d. It declared a tariff on all European Imports.
    e. It forced future presidents to limit their presidencies to two-terms.

116. Which of the following was the impetus for the nullification crisis, in which South Carolina ruled a federal law unconstitutional within its state borders?

    a. The Tariff of 1828
    b. The Fugitive Slave Act
    c. The Missouri Compromise
    d. The Second Bank of the United States
    e. The Second Great Awakening

117. What was significant about the "Revolution of 1800"?

    a. It was a peaceful transition of power between opposing political parties and ideologies.
    b. Democratic-Republicans forced John Adams out of office with force of arms and installed Jefferson.
    c. Democratic-Republicans used nonviolent protest to force a regime change.
    d. The government had to suppress an uprising on the American frontier.
    e. Federalists rebelled after Jefferson's election, and had to be suppressed by the army.

118. Which of the following was the main significance of *Marbury v. Madison*

    a. It established judicial review, allowing the Supreme Court to declare legislation unconstitutional
    b. It was the first time the Supreme Court overturned Congressional legislation
    c. It established federal law as superseding state law
    d. It decreased the power of the Supreme Court to regulate congress
    e. It strengthened the power of the executive branch by explicitly allowing executive orders

119. The Seneca Falls Convention was chiefly concerned with issues of which type?

    a. Women's rights (especially the right to vote)
    b. Religious toleration in the wake of the Second Great Awakening
    c. Inadequacies of the Articles of Confederation
    d. The War of 1812 and international relations with Britain
    e. The immediate enactment of the abolition of slavery

120. Which of the following was a result of the Kansas Nebraska Act?

    a. Kansas was established as a free territory, while Nebraska was established as a slave territory
    b. Kansas and Nebraska were established as free territories and would become free states
    c. Kansas and Nebraska were given the option of voting on whether to become free or slave states
    d. Kansas was established as a slave territory, while Nebraska was established as a free territory
    e. The federal government set up a permanent Native American territory in Kansas and Nebraska.

Answer Key and Explanations

1. E: The 1494 Treaty of Tordesillas predated Balboa's 1513 Panamanian expedition, Cortés's 1519-1521 incursion into the Aztec empire, and Pizarro's 1532 destruction of the Tawantinsuyu.

2. E: Colonial opposition to post-French and Indian War taxes can be summarized by the call, "No taxation without representation!" Colonial legislatures considered it their duty to tax goods in the colonies since they, and not Parliament, were elected by the colonists. England had no written constitution but instead, a commonly agreed upon set of principles and the rich history of precedent. Colonial state charters were written and inflexible, while the English constitution was malleable in the sense that Parliament could pass any law it currently thought necessary to meet the current need. Taxes benefitted untaxed British joint-stock companies such as the East India Company, but hurt local merchants in the colonies. However, both British and colonial troops fought in the French and Indian War, so opposition did not divide the British and the colonists.

3. D: The three plans that were brought up during the Second Constitutional Convention were the New Jersey plan, which favored less populous states; the Virginia plan, which favored more populous states; and the Connecticut plan, which attempted to appeal to both categories of states and provided for two houses of the legislature, one house whose membership was based on the population of the state and the other house made up of an equal number of representatives for all the states.

4. C: Vermont was not one of the original 13 colonies. Massachusetts is represented as part of New England, along with Connecticut, New Hampshire, and Rhode Island, near the head of the snake. Virginia and New York have their own segments, but Georgia (though one of the original 13 colonies) is excluded.

5. E: Salutary neglect refers to Britain's unwritten policy of not enforcing international trade laws for its colonies. The Navigation Act had required the American colonies to only trade with England. All trade goods had to be sent on British ships. If trade was going to another country, the ship had to pass through a British port first in order for a tax or duty to be assessed. A benign blind eye was turned to American foreign trade because it resulted in a higher standard of living in the colonies and therefore more money flowing to Britain. Also, it meant that fewer enforcement officers had to be employed, which saved money. Many of the officials appointed to enforce these laws were also very favorable to local colonial interests and therefore did not put forth much effort to enforce the laws. When this policy was changed and new taxes imposed, the colonies strongly resisted, resulting in the revolutionary war.

6. C: America was a patriarchal society, but the colonists were strong people and everybody had to help. Women were never formally considered for active military duty and in many cases the men might say that the primary role of a married woman with children was to remain home and raise them. However, many of the women with no way to support themselves and no form of protection often followed the army camps and provided what help they could. This help often took the form of nurse, seamstress, cook, maid, launderer, spy, and in some cases, secret soldiers. Those caught impersonating a male soldier were usually imprisoned, though there were a few recorded cases where men assigned to cannon batteries had the aid of their wives with them on the battlefield. Women filled many different roles during the American Revolutionary War.

7. D: American Tories and Redcoats were strongly opposed to the Boston Tea Party, while Quebecois Francophones and Southern farmers were generally indifferent as it didn't impact them

directly. Yankee merchants, however, were directly affected by and hence strongly opposed to the Tea Act, and thus in favor of the Boston Tea Party.

8. B: Cotton and peaches did not become significant in Southern agriculture until the 1800s. Chesapeake Bay tobacco and Carolina rice were major cash crops (along with Indigo) during the colonial period. Most of the food for the nation was grown in the mid-Atlantic colonies. The manufacturing took place in the North East. Because of its long growing season, the South turned to cash crops intended for export.

9. B: The French and Indian War, although a British victory, generated large amounts of war debt for Great Britain. This in turn prompted the British to take a more active role in colonial government, ending salutary neglect and raising taxes in an effort to make the colonies more productive as a source of revenue to retire the debt. It fell predominantly on the American colonies because they were the direct beneficiaries of the British victory. As a result, both the British and the colonists viewed each other differently, and acted less independently. This change in view and practice would lead ultimately to the revolutionary war and American independence.

10. C: This passage is taken from Thomas Paine's *Common Sense* and argues against being entangled with European nations. The sentiments are similar to Washington's reservations about entangling alliances expressed during his farewell address.

11. C: While opposition to trade and taxation came from mercantilism, they are not its core planks. In addition, economic independence and a focus on merchants are, despite the name, not mercantilism. Mercantilism is the view that colonies exist only for the good of their mother countries' benefit.

12. E: The number of American deaths due to the revolutionary war was about 25,000. This was not that high compared to other conflicts in American history. For example the deaths during the Civil War totaled more than 600,000. The revolutionary war losses had little impact on the number of men available for marriage and thus a very small affect (if any) on the birth rates. Many men did cross the Appalachian Mountains and thus significantly impacted the number of never-married women. Many women were also waiting to get married and start their families until later in life. Many women also decided to have smaller families than their mothers had. There was also an increased use of birth control throughout the 19th century which resulted in declining birth rates, particularly in urban areas.

13. A: Americans have traditionally always valued their personal liberty above all. The Dominion of New England stripped colonists of many of their cherished liberties and rights. This angered them greatly. Andros was not a weak leader and he attempted a few reforms, but ultimately it was still too much of a centralized tyrannical government in the eyes of the colonists. There were no economic repercussions for trading, taxation, or related issues. It was primarily about self rule versus centralized power under the king's appointed governor. As soon as James was removed from the British throne, many of the changes were immediately reversed by the colonists.

14. E: All three colonies were founded to shelter minority faiths. - Puritans in Massachusetts, Quakers in Pennsylvania, and Roman Catholics in Maryland. All of the other answer choices have to do with economics. Trade, indebtedness, resources, and other economic matters were not the primary motivation in the formation of these colonies, but as safe havens for their respective religions.

15. D: The federalists were chiefly concerned with the passage of the constitution. Slave States compromised and agreed to have only three-fifths of their slaves count towards representation.

Small states compromised by allowing the House of Representatives to be based upon population. Anti-federalists' concerns over the creation of a "strong" national government were assuaged with the promise of the passage of a bill of rights. Abolitionists compromised by allowing the slave trade to continue for another 20 years.

16. C: The American victory at Saratoga convinced the French that the American cause could be a successful one. Because of this victory, France formally became America's ally and provided direct monetary and military support to the revolution. The battle of Saratoga was not a naval battle, and the Americans were not seeking supplies or gunpowder. The British failed to cut through the American defenses and they retreated to Saratoga, not the sea.

17. C: In the Treaty of Paris (1763) that ended the French and Indian War, France ceded the area east of the Mississippi to Britain. In the Treaty of Paris (1783) that ended the Revolutionary war, the new American nation was granted the land east of the Mississippi. Pinckney's treaty with Spain, which owned Louisiana at the time, assured American navigation rights on the Mississippi river. Prior to the Adams-Onis treaty, Spain claimed the border of Louisiana to be the land west of the Mississippi. The treaty granted the land east of the Sabine River to the United States. Jay's Treaty was negotiated between the Americans and British to resolve issues left over from the revolutionary war. The British were not concerned with the Mississippi river since the issue was specifically handled by the Paris Treaty of 1783.

18. A: Voting in Massachusetts was very limited as well as who could run for office. Reverend Thomas Hooker was dissatisfied with the strict voting laws within Massachusetts, and led a group of about one hundred settlers out of the colony. They formed a new town called Hartford in the Connecticut River valley. They wanted to be self governing and therefore drew up a constitution. Their constitution resembled the government already established in Massachusetts, but extended voting rights to all men.

19. A: Western Pennsylvania had witnessed repeated attacks from Native Americans who were angry at being removed from their lands. The Paxton Boys were a group of Scots-Irish settlers who attacked and killed a group of about 20 Native Americans as reprisal for past attacks. The government of Pennsylvania wanted to put the Paxton Boys on trial for the crime. An angry mob of Scots-Irish settlers marched on Philadelphia as a way to protest the prosecution of the Paxton Boys when the same government would do nothing to protect frontier farms from Native American attacks. Benjamin Franklin was able to calm the mob and the Paxton Boys were not prosecuted. They were very upset about a seemingly indifferent government that would not protect them on the frontier. Abolition, taxation, and revolution were not issues at this time in American history.

20. E: Joseph Smith, Charles Finney, and William Miller were all preachers during the second great awakening in the 1800s. Joseph Smith was the founder of the Church of Jesus Christ of latter day saints (the Mormons). Charles Finney was a Presbyterian minister who preached in New York. Charles Miller started a movement that looked for the return of Jesus Christ at any moment that eventually led to the formation of the Seventh Day Adventist denomination. George Whitefield was a contemporary of Jonathan Edwards. They both preached during the colonial period prior to the revolutionary war. Whitefield was an Anglican minister and started an orphanage in the Georgia colony and preached in many other places in the colonies as well as many places in England. Whitefield was a friend of Benjamin Franklin and the two exchanged many letters. Whitefield preached often in Philadelphia. The meeting house built for Whitefield to preach in eventually became the University of Pennsylvania thanks to Benjamin Franklin. Jonathan Edwards was a Congregationalist minister who preached the famous sermon "Sinners in the Hands of Angry God" on July 8th, 1741. It had a profound effect and was part of the First Great Awakening in America.

This sermon is studied by historians and others to this day. It is a good example of the type of preaching that occurred during the First Great Awakening.

21. A: Washington was able to put down the large rebellion by sending 13,000 troops into Pennsylvania, making B and C incorrect. Because the crises forced federal government action, choice E's statement that it was only a small problem proves false. Washington was able to show that citizens must follow the constitutional laws of the land. However, he never became a heartless leader who ignored the pleas of the citizens, making A the best choice.

22. C: America's main advantage was their knowledge of the terrain and their desire to fight for their homeland. Their knowledge helped them organize guerilla warfare attacks. All of the other choices were ADVANTAGES for the British at the outset of the war.

23. C: The Navigation Acts required goods from the colonies to be shipped by British vessels to British ports, and specified the few goods the colonies were allowed to export (originally, tobacco was the only one on the list). This was intended to promote mercantilism, the system by which the mother country (Great Britain) held colonies solely for its own benefit. The Acts served to promote the economic interests of Britain.

24. A: The Virginia and Kentucky resolutions, which were written by Madison and Jefferson respectively, sought to correct the wrongs imposed by the Alien and Sedition Acts. They argued that because these laws were in disagreement with the constitution, it was the states' duty to declare the laws unconstitutional and not abide by them. Nullification would reach a boiling point later in American History in the 1800s when South Carolina would nullify a Tariff passed by Congress during the presidency of Andrew Jackson.

25. C: Before Grenville became prime minister, British citizens paid more than 5 times the amount of taxes that colonists did. After their success in the Seven Years War, the War of the Austrian Succession, and the War of the Spanish Succession, Britain wanted to expand their empire. These wars also left Britain in debt, leading Grenville to raise taxes on the colonies when he became prime minister.

26. D: Prior to the manumission act, slaves could only be freed by a direct action of the Virginia Assembly. The manumission act allowed slave owners the ability to free their slaves directly. All that was necessary was either a deed of manumission or a last will and testament stating their freedom. By making this change, a slave holder could free their slaves at their own discretion. It was the 15th Amendment to the constitution that gave African Americans the right to vote, not the manumission act. The manumission act had nothing to do with the purchase of slaves or fugitive slave laws.

27. D: The Triangular Trade did not involve the lumber trade or small scale trade in New England or between southern and northern colonies. The Triangle trade was a complex web of trading that involved the American colonies, West Africa, and the Caribbean. Sometimes it included Western Europe, West Africa, and Islands in the Caribbean. America produced agricultural products and raw materials that were exchanged for manufactured goods in Europe, or slaves in West Africa. The Slaves were brought to the Caribbean and traded for sugar, molasses, or rum. The sugar, molasses and sometimes the slaves were brought to the American colonies. These were traded for molasses, rum, or agricultural products. The process would again repeat as each market provided what it could and traded for what it needed. It is named for the relative position of each stop between American, Europe, Africa, and the Caribbean, but also because the sail driven ships found it easier to

cross the Atlantic westward with the "trade winds" (from West Africa to the Caribbean) and return eastward with the easterlies and gulf current (from the Americas to Europe).

28. D: Plantations were largely a Southern phenomenon. Encomiendas were Spanish. Manors were British. Fiefs were medieval divisions of land. Patroonships were the Dutch name for the large tracts of land that New Netherland was divided into.

29. C: Primogeniture was an ancient feudal system law and practice that ensured land owned by the local lord did not become so subdivided by succeeding generations as to become useless for agriculture. Therefore, all the land would be inherited by the oldest legitimate male heir (oldest son). This practice was transposed from Britain to the American colonies. It was particularly popular in the mid-Atlantic and southern states where large plantations prevailed. However, it fell out of favor because it tended to breed an aristocracy who controlled land, money, power, and local politics. It also seemed unnecessary given the huge amount of land available to the west (as long as you didn't consider the Native Americans already living there.) It was eventually abolished throughout America so that the land owner was free to dispose of his land as he wished.

30. A: Anti-Federalists were opposed to all forms of a strong central government. They feared the tyranny of an executive who would act like a king and deprive the citizens and states of their rights and freedoms. Therefore, they would not sign or support the constitution until a bill of rights had been added to it to protect the liberties, rights, and freedoms of the individual citizens. Anti-Federalists were in favor of decentralization, state's rights, and willing cooperation rather than enforced, coercive, centralized power. They preferred this, even if it meant a country that was weaker and struggled to defend itself and made international affairs less efficient.

31. D: The painting depicts General George Washington crossing the Delaware River on December 25, 1776. The crossing took place at night and was supposed to one of three separate crossings. Only General Washington's group was able to make the crossing successfully. The other two crossings were thwarted by ice and weather. The river crossing took place during a strong winter storm and landed over three hours later than Washington had planned. He went forward with the attack on the Hessian garrison in Trenton, New Jersey. Thanks to Washington's large number of artillery pieces and tenacity, he was able to win the battle. This famous painting was done by Emanuel Leutze a German artist, in 1851. The painting is now displayed at the Metropolitan Museum of Art in New York City.

32. C: Thomas Jefferson used the political philosophy of John Locke to argue that government's power is derived from the consent of the governed when he placed that phrase in the declaration of independence. Locke argued for this position in his work called "Two Treatises on Government". He states that each person has a natural right to protect their freedom and property (life, liberty, and estate). Each individual gives up that individual right to a group. When giving that individual right to the group, Locke argues, that the individual has consented. Therefore, government is a group that consents to collective protection of their property (life, liberty, estate). David Hume argued against this position and stated that nowhere does a government exist that is truly the universal consent of the governed and thus there is some partial tyranny or use of power to force those who do not consent to remain.

33. A: The Boston Massacre happened when a squad of British soldiers came to the aid of a British sentry who was being heckled and having snowballs thrown at him. The British soldiers fired on the hecklers and 3 died. The event helped galvanize American colonists against the British and in favor of independence. The Townshend Acts and Declaratory Act had to do with taxation and happened prior to the Boston Massacre (1766 and 1767). They were not the result of it. The Boston

Tea Party happened after the Boston Massacre and therefore cannot be viewed as proof of its ineffectiveness. It also did not increase loyalty to the British crown, but in fact helped diminish it and promote revolutionary sentiments.

34. E: The New England family lifestyle involved dividing a father's land among all of his sons, not just the eldest. As families remained on the same land for generations, the parcels allotted to each son got smaller and smaller. The communities were small and close knit. Their religious beliefs tended to be very strong due to their puritan theology. However, New England retained a rigid class system. This was inherited from the British culture and was strongly entrenched in the colonies.

35. D: King Philip's war was fought when the Native Americans of New England attempted to retake land from the colonists. One of the factors in Bacon's rebellion was lack of government protection from Native American raids against the Virginia frontier. Lord Dunmore's War was against the Shawnee who wanted to drive white settlers off of their hunting ground in the Ohio River valley.

36. B: Many of the prisons in England were overcrowded with people failing to pay their debts. To help alleviate this problem, the British government issued a royal charter to James Oglethorpe and other philanthropists to allow these prisoners to start over in the New World. Many of the debtors were not well equipped for the hard life of clearing land and farming. They struggled to produce a thriving colony because there was less incentive, less capital, and fewer people with the necessary skills to be successful.

37. D: The passage is taken from the Flushing Remonstrance, a 1657 petition to Peter Stuyvesant, the governor of New Netherland, requesting exemption from a ban on Quaker worship. The statement's request for religious tolerance is most clearly consistent with the First Amendment's statement of freedom of religion.

38. B: Charles II is the king who granted royal charters to Connecticut and Rhode Island. Some who lived in older colonies (like Massachusetts) chafed under the strict puritan order. They moved out to new land and negotiated treaties with the Native Americans. Once these colonies were established, their neighbors wanted to incorporate them back into the already existing colony. Fearing a return to what they had originally wanted to get away from, they appealed to King Charles II. He granted their charters along with some of the strongest freedoms and liberties of any colony.

39. A: Roger Williams was the founder of Rhode Island after he was expelled from Massachusetts for his strong views of the freedom of conscience in religious matters. As founder of Rhode Island he worked hard to articulate religious tolerance and a separation of church and state so that each person could worship and believe according to the dictates of their own conscience.

40. B: Nowhere in the Articles of Confederation did it call for an executive branch for the United States government. The citizens of this new country would not have been too eager to be under the rule of a person with so much power after fighting a war to overthrow King George III.

41. B: The Whiskey Rebellion was quickly suppressed with little bloodshed, after Washington amassed about 13,000 troops. It was put down much more effectively than Shays' Rebellion under the Articles of Confederation. However, the government's opponents, such as Thomas Jefferson, criticized the response as authoritarian and unwarranted action against small farmers.

42. B: Hamilton wanted to create a nation that was an industrial superpower. He also planned for the Federal government to assume the states' debts from the revolutionary war in order to bolster confidence in America's credit worthiness. He did this so that the United States would be

- 91 -

recognized and respected by the countries of Europe. He also favored a pro-British foreign and trade policy as opposed to Jefferson's pro-French view.

43. A: The 1754 Siege of Fort Necessity was one of the first battles of the French and Indian War. The 1763 Treaty of Paris ended the French and Indian war. The 1764 Sugar Act was designed to raise money to help repay debt from the war. Opposition to the various means Britain sought to recoup war costs from the colonies led to the 1770 Boston Massacre. Each of these events was a stepping stone on the way to the revolutionary war.

44. C: Christopher Columbus explored the Caribbean in 1492. Ponce de Leon explored Florida in 1513. In 1538, Hernando de Soto explored the areas that today would correspond to Florida, Georgia, Alabama (the North American Southeast). Vasco Nunez de Balboa explored Central America in 1513 (primarily Panama). Francisco Vazquez de Coronado explored the North American Southwest in 1540.

45. A: France wanted control of islands in the Caribbean as a source of sugar. It hoped by helping America with the revolution it might gain British Islands as part of the peace process after the war. Lumber and tobacco were American colonial commodities. The French did not want to take these from its ally. They also had their own sources of fur and gunpowder.

46. B: The Enlightenment had a profound impact on Europe. The founding fathers of the U.S. were strongly influence by it. The U.S. constitution reflects enlightenment ideas. One of the most central tenets of enlightenment thought centers on individual liberty. This is seen in the Bill of Rights. Government's task is not to give its citizens rights, but to protect the individual rights of the citizens that they possess intrinsically. Many of the other answers can be found in the personal opinions of some of the founding fathers, but they are not enshrined in the Constitution. For example, George Washington warned against getting entangled in European conflicts, but that personal sentiment is not in the Constitution. Many of the founding fathers believed that only the wealthy and well educated should lead and have power, however, that is also not found explicitly in the Constitution. The intrinsic liberty of the individual is a strong enlightenment value and is enshrined in the Constitution's Bill of Rights.

47. E: Different colonies were founded by different groups for different reasons. Some were founded on a desire for religious freedom (like Plymouth colony). However, even though these groups were fleeing religious persecution, they did not believe in being tolerant to other groups. They wanted freedom, but only for their particular faith. Puritan New England was staunchly anti-Catholic. Some of the colonies, like Virginia, made the Anglican Church the established faith for the colony. It was supported directly with tax dollars. Other groups had to get permission to form churches. Other faiths were not allowed to worship openly, and adherents to those faiths were forbidden to run for public office. However, there were some colonies established with greater tolerance, like Pennsylvania, Rhode Island, and Maryland. But even in these colonies, some were excluded. Religious life in the colonies was very diverse, but also very sectarian, as each group tended to favor those of their own denomination to the exclusion of others. Jews and Roman Catholics (along with atheists and other minority faiths) struggled to find places to worship freely, and were often barred from running for public office.

48. B: The Necessary and Proper Clause is part of Article One of the Constitution which establishes the legislative branch of government and the powers of Congress. It states that Congress has the power to pass any legislation that is "necessary and proper" for the fulfilling of its enumerated powers in the Constitution. Strict constructionists like Thomas Jefferson understood these words in a very narrow way. Congress could only pass laws related to its enumerated powers that were

absolutely necessary to the fulfilling of those obligations. All other power went to the states per the 10th amendment. However, Federalists, like Alexander Hamilton, argued that it granted "implied powers" to Congress to do what was necessary as long as it was related in some way to one of its enumerated powers. This was used in the argument over whether or not Congress could establish a Federal Bank (or Bank of the United States, chartered by the U.S. government). Federalist would say, yes, Congress has that power. Anti-Federalist would say, no. Because the Federalists carried the day and had support from the Supreme Court in Marbury v. Madison, the implied powers of the Necessary and Proper Clause have led some to call it the "elastic clause", because it is "elastic" or stretchy enough to allow lots of different types of legislation not explicitly enumerated in the Constitution.

49. C: The French revolution was a reaction against an uncaring aristocracy by the common people who desired equality, liberty, and brotherhood (égalité, Liberté, fraternité). It overthrew the monarchy and sought to establish a Constitutional Republic; both things which were true of America and its revolution against Great Britain. This led Americans to favor the revolution in France because they had similar ends in view. However, the French revolution became extremely bloody and radicalized. This caused Americans to disagree with the methods employed while still being in general favor of the goals of the revolution.

50. A: Edmond "Citizen" Genêt, a French ambassador to the United States appointed by the Girondin faction of the French Revolutionary government, attempted to recruit American sailors as privateers to attack British ships. He worked to draw America into the conflict between Britain and France on the side of the French. This was contrary to Washington's strict policy of neutrality in European conflicts. Washington asked the French to remove him from office. Genêt knew that if he returned home he would be executed by the radical Jacobins, who had seized power from the more moderate Girondin faction. Facing execution at home, Genêt was granted asylum in the United States. He married, became a U.S. citizen, and took up farming.

51. E: The Northwest Ordinances of the mid-1780s took land ceded by other original colonies and stipulated how they would be divided up, organized, and brought into the union as equal states. It covered the area that is called the mid-west today (largely in Ohio, Indiana, Illinois, Michigan, and Wisconsin). At the time it was called the Northwest Territory. Oregon and what we think of as the Pacific Northwest would not enter America until the 1800s. The question of slavery in the territories would continue to be a problem until the end of the Civil war and the passage of the 13th, 14th, and 15th amendments to the Constitution. The Northwest Ordinance specifically stipulated that any land acquired from Native Americans must be obtain lawfully through treaty and mutual agreement. The Native Americans were to be protected and treated fairly. The land was already claimed as part of existing states, so it didn't increase the land holdings or size of the U.S. as the Louisiana Purchase did. The Congress under the articles of Confederation prior to the U.S. constitution was weak and often ineffective. However, the organization, division, and sale of the Northwest Territory was one of its most significant accomplishments.

52. A: George Washington and Benjamin Franklin both signed the Constitution but were never accused of being British Loyalists. Samuel Adams and Patrick Henry were never accused of being British Loyalists, and they didn't sign the Constitution. However, John Dickinson both signed the Constitution and was accused of being a British Loyalist. He was the author of *Letters from a Farmer in Pennsylvania* that helped inflame patriotic fervor in the Colonies. However, at the meeting where the Declaration of Independence was drafted and signed, Dickinson called for renewed efforts to reconcile with Britain. He drafted many documents calling for reconciliation such as the Olive Branch Petition sent to King George III. Because of his attempts to reconcile with Britain and his refusal to sign the Declaration of Independence, he was accused of being a British Loyalist.

However, he served in the Continental army and rose to the rank of Brigadier General. He helped draft the articles of Confederation as well as the U.S. Constitution. He was a moderate voice amidst men and times that were not moderate.

53. B: The Stamp Act was the first time a British legislature tried to make money from taxation; all other taxes on the colonies served as economic controls. The Stamp Act was also among the first acts to unite the colonies, since it affected virtually all colonists. It prompted the creation of a namesake assembly in New York, and saw the first major protests by the new Sons of Liberty. Patrick Henry's Virginia resolutions were also a response to the Stamp Act.

54. C: The Middle Passage was the journey from West Africa to the Americas (Brazil, Caribbean, or America). Africans from various regions of western Africa would be kidnapped or captured in battle by other African groups. These captured or kidnapped people would then be marched to the coast and sold to European slave traders for guns, rum, and other goods. The slaves would be packed as tightly as possible into the holds of the sailing ships. There was little to no ventilation, disease was rampant, and many deaths occurred. The dead would be thrown overboard to be consumed by the sharks that often followed the slave ships on their journey across the Atlantic. The journey took between 6 weeks and several months. Food and water were sparingly given to the slaves. They were beaten and abused on the journey in hopes of delivering compliant and broken slaves to the various plantation owners in Brazil, the Caribbean, and America. The slaves would be traded for raw materials like Sugar and agricultural products that would then be sold in Europe for manufactured goods to be traded for slaves in West Africa.

55. B: The First Great Awakening had a profound effect on the colonies. Not only was religion increased as people described religious experiences and conversions, but so was education (new colleges were founded). African American slaves were being evangelized and drawn to the message of Christianity (but there were not many calls for their freedom except from the Quakers). However, there was a great deal of conflict too. Older structures were made to change and give way to a new, more democratic way of thinking. The older, hierarchical denominations saw people leave and join the new more democratic denominations, primarily the Baptists. This was a huge shake up to old established social structures. It was caught up in the spirit of the age that valued the individual and equality over strong class distinctions and a top down authority structure. Many good things came from it, but it also produced a great deal of strife and conflict between social classes and the usual disagreement between the older established ways and new forms and modes in religion and society.

56. C: In the XYZ Affair, three French businessmen whose names were removed from the American diplomatic report and replaced by the letters X, Y, and Z demanded bribes from American diplomats prior to arranging a meeting with the Foreign Minister of France, Talleyrand. He had refused to meet with the American diplomatic delegation because of the pro-British stance of the Federalists. The French were upset with American favor for Britain because of the signing of the Jay treaty. France started to capture American trade ships and antagonize the young country in other ways. When news of the demand for a bribe was made known to the public, outrage increased to the point that some in Congress and the Federal government called for open warfare with France. A naval conflict did ensue between America and France but no formal war was declared (leading to this conflict being called the "Quasi War"). Napoleon came to power shortly thereafter and negotiated a new treaty and an end to the Quasi War.

57. D: The Intolerable Acts did 5 things: closed Boston's port until repayment had been made for all the destroyed tea from the Boston Tea Party, Massachusetts could only hold one town meeting a year and the governor and/or parliament appointed all government officials, British officials were

immune to criminal prosecution in Massachusetts, British troops' had to be quartered on demand in any colony, and they allowed Roman Catholics in Quebec to worship freely. These activities (except for the one related to Quebec) were a direct retaliation for the Boston Tea Party by the Sons of Liberty. The Quebec portion of the acts were disliked because Protestant America did not like having Roman Catholics openly worshipping and tolerated in Southern Canada so close to them. Parliament hoped that the acts would scare other colonies into abandoning Massachusetts and towing the line as loyal British subjects so that similar actions would not befall them. However, instead of isolating Massachusetts, other colonies were roused to strong and direct support of them and were inflamed with strongly negative sentiments toward Britain.

58. A: Benjamin Banneker was a free African American who was born in Maryland. His only formal training was at a Quaker school while still young. He had to drop out of school in order to take over running his family farm. He was a voracious reader and the rest of his education was self taught. He was naturally adept at math and through studying a pocket watch he was given he was able to construct a clock entirely made from wood. He carved all the gears by hand. He also taught himself astronomy and used that knowledge to write and publish an almanac for many years. He corresponded with Thomas Jefferson about slavery and asked him to help bring an end to its practice. He is quoted as having written: "Ah, why will men forget that they are brethren?"

59. D: The land around the colony was very fertile. Jamestown's tobacco crop was one of the few reasons why the colony was able to eventually thrive. The wet, swampy, marsh land where they built the colony bred mosquitoes and disease. Malaria and dysentery from the mosquitoes and the settlers' unpreparedness for the cold winter wiped out a large portion of Jamestown's population. In addition, Jamestown struggled to flourish because of poor trade relationships with the Native Americans and the colonists' refusal to do physical work. One colonist said that they would rather starve than farm. Many of them did. Most of the original colonists were not farmers, but jewelers, and gold and silver smiths. They spent the majority of their time looking for gold. John Smith saved many of them by forcing them to spend a minimum of 4 hours each day farming so that there would be food.

60. A: Most modern historians believe that a land bridge connecting Siberia and Alaska appeared during the last Ice Age when sea levels were lower. Hunter-gatherers followed herds of animals across this land bridge into North America. From there, they spread across the Americas. Christopher Columbus came to the Caribbean in 1492 which sparked the Columbian exchange and started the imperial conquest of the New World by Europeans.

61. A: Taylor ran for the Whig party and Cass ran for the Democratic party. Locofocos (the name for a self lighting match) was the derogatory name applied to Democrats who opposed Democratic president Martin Van Buren in 1840. During the election of 1848 the Free Soilers supported former president Martin Van Buren. The Anti Masons were America's first third party and merged with the Whigs as the group formed.

62. A: In 1812 the governor of Massachusetts signed a bill allowing the state legislature to draw electoral districts in a way beneficial to the Democratic - Republican Party. The shape of the South Essex district was said to look like a salamander and a Boston newspaper used the above cartoon to ridicule the process. Combining the name of the governor of Massachusetts with part of the word salamander, the term Gerrymander was invented. It describes the process of drawing electoral districts for political advantage.

63. B: *Marbury v. Madison* establish the principle of judicial review mentioned in choice D. *McCulloch v. Maryland* ruled that states cannot interfere in the operations of the federal

government. *Gibbons v. Ogden* ruled the Commerce Clause of the Constitution extended to navigation. Though choices C, D, and E correspond individually to the three cases listed, none applies to all three. Rather, the best answer is B. In all three cases the court upheld the supremacy of the federal government over the states.

64. C: One major strategic objective of the Union during the Civil War was to cut off Southern access to the Mississippi River as a conduit for its goods. Cincinnati relied upon river transport for its pork products while Chicago's economy relied upon the railroad. During the Civil War, Chicago's means of transportation was unhindered while Cincinnati lost access to the river for more than two years during the war.

65. D: The American Party also known as the "Know-Nothing" party, was a xenophobic, nativist party. They believed that the slavery issue was created by political insiders to distract from the large numbers of incoming immigrants. They supported the idea that there was a Catholic plot to undermine democracy in America. Cheap immigrant laborers, who could facilitate the means of mass production, most threatened the skilled artisans they could replace. Protestant artisans were the mostly likely group to have supported the American Party.

66. C: John Tyler was never known for moral laxity. When Tyler was elected to the Vice Presidency in 1840, he had been a Whig for six years, but prior to that had been a Democrat and still hewed towards Democratic positions on issues such as states' rights. The fact that he never fully belonged to either party left him without allies in Washington and left many suspicious of him when he assumed the Presidency. To compound that suspicion, the Constitution was vague in delineating presidential succession. Many wondered whether Tyler inherited the actual office of the Presidency or merely the powers and duties associated with it.

67. E: Mexico achieved it's independence in 1821 and Texas declared its independence from Mexico in 1835. Though in general Texans wanted their territory to be annexed, there was about a decade's delay due to fears that the annexation would spark a war. The U.S. annexed Texas in 1845, which did help spark the Mexican-American war in which Mexico was defeated and it signed the Treaty of Guadalupe-Hidalgo in February 1848.

68. A: The canal was built prior the surge in growth of the railroads and even competed successfully with them once they came into their prime. It was built to connect Lake Erie with the Hudson River in order to move products from inland areas and get them to New York Harbor. Prior to this, goods were sent down the Mississippi River through New Orleans. The canal dramatically shortened the time and the cost of moving goods to the coast in order to be shipped abroad. It was not meant to help move Canadian products to America, but American products from the interior to the coast in order to be shipped overseas. It was so successful that it led to an economic boom and promoted a huge increase in population for the region.

69. A: The Missouri Compromise was passed in 1820 and stated that slavery would not exist north of the 36°30' parallel (except for Missouri) to help determine the issue of whether new territories should enter the union as free or slave states. Nat Turner's rebellion was put down in 1831. The Wilmot Proviso, although it was never adopted, was an amendment to an appropriations bill proposed for the first time in 1846 that would have banned slavery in any territory gained from Mexico after the Mexican-American War. Lincoln was chosen to be president in 1860 and was elected without the support of a single slave state. Fears regarding the banning of slavery led to the secession of the southern states, the formation of the confederacy, and the beginning of the civil war.

70. D: The most important reason for the 1860 split in the Democratic Party was Douglas' moderate view on slavery and the subsequent unwillingness of the radical, pro-slavery, Fire-Eaters to accept him as a nominee. While Douglas did advocate for a transcontinental railroad that would run through the North (and originate in his home state of Illinois), this was not nearly as important as the all-consuming slavery issue.

71. E: Land in Arizona, Colorado, and California were a part of the Mexican cession of 1848. Parts of what is now southern Louisiana (east of the Sabine river) were ceded as part of the Adams-Onis treaty of 1819. The entirety of present day Missouri was a part of the Louisiana Purchase of 1803.

72. C: From 1830-1860, all other regions listed contributed at least 200,000 immigrants to the United States, while Eastern European immigration to the US during this period was negligible.

73. E: The 36°30' line is the Missouri Compromise line and currently borders on Missouri, Arkansas, Texas, and Oklahoma. The 54°40' line was a source of controversy during the election of 1844 (it was the northernmost claim by the U.S., while Britain claimed as far south as 42°). It was ceded to Britain and the northern border of the US was set at 49°. The 39°43' line is the Pennsylvania-Maryland border surveyed by Mason and Dixon.

74. C: While John Brown did lead abolitionist militants during the conflict in Kansas in 1856, the raid on Harpers Ferry occurred in October of 1859. In the immediate aftermath of the raid, John Brown's actions were condemned by observers in both the North and the South. John Brown only became popular in the North during his trial some weeks later. John Brown intended to use the weapons to arm a slave revolt, and while the raid itself contributed to the sectional tensions that would lead to the Civil War, that was not John Brown's intention. He was motivated exclusively by ideology.

75. D: The Second Great Awakening was a Protestant movement of religious revival that began in the last years of the 18th century and continued into the mid 19th century. As participation in religious groups rose, Church members began to apply religious teachings to problems afflicting society. Participants in the Second Great Awakening tried to reform prisons, improve treatment for the mentally ill, fight against the proliferation of alcohol, and work for additional rights for both women and African Americans.

76. D: Missouri was added as a slave state and it was desirable to balance it with the admission of a free state. Both Arkansas and Alabama are south of Missouri and entered the union as slave states. Kansas entered the union as part of 1854's Kansas-Nebraska Act. Michigan entered the union in 1837. Maine was admitted along with Missouri in 1820.

77. B: The Hudson River School was a movement that depicted the beauty of America's untouched wilderness during the mid 19th century. At that time, the United States was not a world power, its industries had not yet developed, and virtually the entire nation was rural. Artists from the Hudson River Group like Thomas Cole and Asher Durand focused on the indisputable natural beauty of the American wilderness.

78. C: In 1831 Alexis de Tocqueville and Gustave de Beaumont were sent by the French government to investigate the American prison system. Based on his visit, de Tocqueville wrote Democracy in America including his observations on many different aspects of its culture, including women.

79. E: Whitney is best remembered for his invention of the Cotton Engine (shortened to "Gin") and his advocacy for interchangeable parts. Whitney received an order for 10,000 muskets for the U.S. government to be produced in two years. Up to that point, muskets had been handmade

individually, making their production very slow. However, Whitney was able to fill the order by standardizing each part and then mass producing 10,000 copies of every part, advancing the development of mass production greatly.

80. B: African Americans did not found their own churches until after the Civil War, so concentration of African American churches can be ruled out. Factories were not prevalent in the south prior to the Civil War and Tobacco was not grown in the deep South (Louisiana, Mississippi, Alabama, and Georgia). However, cotton was produced in those areas and high yields of cotton required larger populations of slaves to grow and process the crops.

81. E: While it is true that the British did seize Washington D.C. and burn the White House, they did so after the War of 1812 started and therefore could not be considered a reason to go to war with Britain in 1812. Jefferson's Embargo Act did lead to a decline in a previously prospering economy focused on trade with Britain and France, and combined with the British impressment of American sailors, roused the American public against Britain. War hawks (from the South and West) in Congress strongly advocated for war. They felt this way because the British were arming and encouraging the Native Americans on the Frontier to attack American settlements. War was also seen as an opportunity for America to invade Canada and "free" it from British control.

82. D: The Era of Good feelings is associated with the presidency of James Monroe. During his term in office, the last Federalist Presidential Candidate, Rufus King, ran against Monroe, marking the end of the first party system. James Monroe was the third of the three consecutive presidents from Virginia (Jefferson, Madison, Monroe). President Monroe favored the Back-to-Africa Movement as an alternative to abolition. The larger abolition movement would become more prominent later in the 19th century.

83. D: A gag rule is a rule passed by a legislative body that prevents a particular topic from being introduced, discussed, or acted upon. Specifically, the U.S. Congress passed a gag rule to prevent the issue of slavery to be brought up, discussed, considered, or acted upon. This was in response to the myriads of petitions that poured into both the House and the Senate from Northern Abolitionists. The right of the people of the U.S. to petition their government was effectively being nullified by the Congressional Rule. It was eventually repealed. However, the issue of slavery would not be finally settled until the end of the Civil War and the passage of the 13th amendment to the Constitution.

84. B: Gold was found at Sutter's Mill in early 1848. Communication was much slower during the 19th century and it took time for the news to spread, but by the next year, huge numbers of young men were doing everything they could to get the resources together to make the arduous journey to California with the hopes of getting fabulously wealthy. They borrowed huge sums of money to get the equipment and passage necessary to get to California over land or by sea. Disease on the trail, as well as hostile Native Americans, storms, and other difficulties faced those who went out West. Many never survived the trek to California. However, those who did survive the journey found it difficult to secure a place to prospect and protect it from others. There was fraud and theft, and many different ways for the prospectors to lose all their possessions or even their lives. The Gold rush hit its peak in 1852 and was starting to decline significantly by the late 1850s. Most never got rich, but this event forever marked America and changed the course for California which started it life as a sparsely populated territory and ended up as a very diverse and populous state.

85. D: The phrase "with malice towards none, with charity for all" was included in Lincoln's Second Inaugural Address. His plan for reconstruction was a lenient one wishing above all to heal the breach in the country and bring the union back together again. He is quoted as saying "If I could save the Union without freeing any slave I would do it, and if I could save it by freeing all the slaves I

- 98 -

would do it; and if I could save it by freeing some and leaving others alone I would also do that." He believed this to be his official duty as president of the United States. He wrote: "I would save the Union." But he also wrote that it was his "oft-expressed personal wish that all men everywhere could be free." Johnson was a Southerner from Tennessee, and would not have advocated for full and absolute equality for freed slaves. He wrote: "This is a country for white men, and by God, as long as I am president, it shall be a government for white men." Though he didn't favor slavery, he also did not favor equality between whites and African Americans. The Democratic Party at the time was split between northern and southern factions and did not have a unified plan. Henry Clay had died in 1852 before the outbreak of the Civil War. Congress, controlled by the Republicans, was the group that put forth a plan that sought to bring about political and economic equality for the recently freed African American slaves. Congress controlled reconstruction until 1877.

86. A: The Ostend Manifesto was part of President Pierce's attempt to increase American holdings in the Caribbean. The document laid out reasons why American would be justified in taking Cuba away from Spain by force. It was hoped that Spain would sell Cuba to America, but if they refused, then this document was to serve as the rationale for invading and taking Cuba through military force. When the manifesto became public in 1855, northerners perceived it as part of the southern conspiracy aimed at gaining additional slave colonies. Voting rights would not be a big issue until after the Civil War. Manifest Destiny (answer choice C) had already been achieved with the Mexican Cession in 1848.

87. E: The Louisiana Purchase was concluded in 1803, several years after the end of the Quasi War with France, and the Gadsden Purchase was negotiated in 1853, several years after the end of the Mexican-American War. The constitutionality of Thomas Jefferson's purchase of Louisiana was questioned, but the Gadsden Purchase was not. The Louisiana Purchase gave United States full access to the Mississippi River, and significantly increased the area of the United States. However, the Gadsden Purchase did not involve navigable waterways like the Mississippi River in the Louisiana Purchase. Also, the Gadsden Purchase did not double the size of the U.S. like the Louisiana Purchase did. However, the Gadsden Purchase was completed with the aim to use the land to facilitate the building of a transcontinental railroad across the South. No such infrastructure improvement was planned for the Louisiana Purchase.

88. A: The 1816 Tariff was designed to protect industry, not merely raise revenue. The telegraph had not yet been invented. Included in the proposal that became known as the American System, was the goal of creating a Navy, which would involve increased defense spending. And central to the whole system was the formation of a National Bank.

89. E: Horace Mann was the superintendent of the Massachusetts board of education, where he changed the curriculum to more practically useful subjects such as arithmetic and physical science instead of classical literature. He also extended the school year to 6 months and pushed for increased attendance among middle class children. He was instrumental in Educational Reform.

90. C: Whitman wrote the 206-line elegy during the period of mourning that followed the assassination of President Lincoln. Though the poem never mentions Lincoln by name, he uses pastoral nature imagery to depict the sorrow of death. Through the use of drooping flowers, the setting of the morning star (Venus) and other images, he describes the sense of loss, the struggle to deal with grief, and then the final acceptance of death. It includes allusions to the Civil War, though the war itself is never named. The poem is full of pathos and powerful imagery to fire the imagination and help the reader enter the sense of loss, grief, and ultimately acceptance that Whitman hoped to convey.

91. B: The Dred Scott case came well after the Free Soil Party began and therefore could not be a reason for its formation. Land prices and Mexican counterattack were not significant factors in the formation of the party. Any moral opposition to slavery was greatly overshadowed by the fear that Free African Americans, and enslaved African Americans would be able to do work for less money and therefore undercut non-slave owning farmers and merchants. It was sometimes criticized as being no more than "white manism". Their slogan was "Free soil, Free speech, Free labor, and Free men". They opposed the expansion of slavery into the new western territories, but primarily on economic and not moral grounds. They had a more moderate view on slavery compared to the radical abolitionists. They believed that if slavery did not expand, then it would eventually die out and be seen as backward and outmoded. Some may have believed that it was immoral, but that was not the primary view of their political party.

92. D: Francis Scott Key originally wrote "The Star-Spangled Banner" as a poem while imprisoned on a British ship as it bombarded Fort McHenry. He noted the brave tenacity of its defenders, incorporating that into the poem that would later be set to music and be chosen as the American national anthem.

93. D: A period of rapid growth, easy lending policies at banks, and runaway land speculation was followed by steep deflation and banking practices that increased interest rates, and made acquiring loans more difficult. Many lost their farms, businesses failed, and unemployment rose sharply. The other events might (and did in some cases) involve short term and localized panic, but the economic downturn of the late 1830 was felt worldwide.

94. E: The Waltham-Lowell System was a system that incorporated all aspects of textile production in one mill. They were located along rivers to provide power from the water. The mills often became towns as they provided company housing as well as a company store. These mill towns hired local young women. They worked 14 hour days, 6 days a week. The local dormitories they lived in had strict rules and were overseen by older women. Though it was a difficult life, it did provide many women work and opportunities to gain financial independence.

95. B: The American South had a warm climate and a long growing season. It was ideal for many different cash crops, like indigo and rice. Tobacco was a difficult crop that rapidly removed nutrients from the soil. But if done well, it could generate large sums of money. However, with the invention of the cotton gin, and the growth of textile mills in Britain and the Northeastern U.S., cotton became an extremely lucrative crop. Because cotton was easy to grow and didn't deplete the soil, most farmers in the South readily switch to growing cotton instead of tobacco.

96. D: The Tariff was the first protective tariff passed by the U.S. government in order to protect American manufacturers from inexpensive British goods. The British did not need to pay their workers as well as the U.S. did. That, coupled with inexpensive raw materials, allowed the British to produce quality products at very low prices. In order for American made products to compete the price of the British goods had to be increased. The Tariff was meant to accomplish this goal.

97. B: John Quincy Adams's personality did not endear him to others. He was irritable and reserved in his dealings with those around him. He became president through what has become known as the "corrupt bargain" with Henry Clay. Those of the opposition party had a strong reason to dislike him for this deal. It made him unpopular in the eyes of the public because it looked like he had stolen the election from Andrew Jackson who won the popular vote but couldn't garner enough electoral college votes to win the election. John Quincy Adams opposed the removal of Native Americans from their land. Those who wanted those lands were upset that he protected the right of the Native Americans to remain on the land. Because he promoted Federal funding for

- 100 -

infrastructure improvements, many felt that the federal government was intruding into something that was the purview of the states. State's rights advocates disliked his administration for this reason. However, he was in favor of eliminating the "spoils system" and employing government workers based on merit and not merely based on being a political ally. Those who favored an end to the spoils system were happy to see him in opposition to this.

98. D: The speech was given to help promote the compromise of 1850. California had been ceded after the Mexican-American war and was petitioning to become a state. Their state constitution outlawed slavery. Admitting California as a free state that outlawed slavery would upset the balance in the senate and so the southern states would never allow California to come into the union. This would seem to stymie manifest destiny. Daniel Webster and Henry Clay both supported compromise to resolve the conflict and forestall succession and war. The compromise of 1850 involved several different things, all aimed at different factions in congress and in the nation. It outlawed the slave trade (though not slavery itself) in the nation's capital, Washington, D.C. It admitted California as a free state. It settled a border dispute between Texas and New Mexico and promised to take on Texas' debt. It enacted a much stronger fugitive slave law and put enforcement in the hands of the Federal Government instead of the states. And it left the newly formed territories of Utah and New Mexico to decide the question of slavery for themselves (Popular sovereignty). Everybody got something they wanted, but at the price of having to accept something they didn't want.

99. B: Jackson's presidency is sometimes referred to as the Era of the Common Man. Voting rights were extended to include voters who were not wealthy landowners (though still only to white men; women and minorities were not yet allowed to vote). For the first time middle class men voted and supported the candidate with whom they identified. Jackson's humble origins and status as a political outsider allowed him to tap into populist sentiment and win the election against more affluent opponents.

100. A: Sharecropping emerged as a mechanism for Southern land owners to maintain their sources of labor and continue to control freed slaves. Since freed slaves had no work, and the former slave-owners needed a labor force for their plantations, freed slaves would continue to work for their former owners. However, in return for land and tools, the freedman would have to give up a portion of his harvest, and would often get paid in currency only usable on a specific plantation. This system kept freedmen economically dependent and socially inferior.

101. A: The National Bank helped stabilize the currency which appealed to merchants. Eastern aristocrats, due to their wealth, had influence over the economy. This power was partially exercised through the Bank. Western Farmers were opposed to the Bank because it regulated interest rates, the availability of loans, and often foreclosed on farms. This lead to farmers seeing the bank as a necessary evil, but one they didn't care for.

102. C: The putting-out system was a manufacturing arrangement utilized in the early United States before the rise of centralized factories. Also known as the cottage industry, raw materials and machines were employed by individual families to produce finished products such as shoes. Cottage industries were particularly attractive to farming families who had both the time and desire for additional family income.

103. D: The Trail of Tears moved Native Americans from Georgia to Oklahoma and therefore had nothing to do with the debate regarding slavery. The advent of universal white male suffrage was not primarily concerned with slaves. The demise of the National Bank and the Panic of 1837 were both financial in nature and did not directly impinge upon slavery. However, the annexation of

Texas was opposed largely because of opposition to the expansion of slavery into a new southern territory. Due to sectionalism and the constant power struggles to prevent free or slave states from having a majority in the Senate caused constant strife as each new state was incorporated into the union. Often, they had to come in pairs, one slave, one free, to maintain the balance.

104. A: Stephen Douglas was the only candidate to actively campaign during the election of 1860. While the election did showcase the Republicans' dominance in the North and West that would last for decades to come, they failed to win any states in the South. Modern campaign structures, organization, and tactics were not employed until the election of 1896, Kansas and Nebraska could not vote until the 1864 and 1868 elections, respectively, and the Whig Party had already died out six years prior.

105. C: The Federalists no longer existed in 1840. The Whigs believed in government spending on internal improvements, while the Democrats opposed it. From its beginnings, the Democrats were the party of farmers. They were opposed to the power of big banks.

106. B: The Emancipation Proclamation was issued in 1863 after the outbreak of the Civil War. Calhoun's 1828 "South Carolina Exposition and Protest" related to the nullification of a federal tariff and therefore did not lead directly to the Civil War. The Tenth amendment to the constitution was a part of the Bill of Rights in 1789. The Wilmot Proviso of 1846 sought to prohibit the expansion of slavery to any land acquired as a result of the Mexican-American War. Lincoln delivered his House Divided Speech in 1858 and was unequivocally against a divided United States. Lincoln said, "I believe this government cannot endure, permanently, half slave and half free. I do not expect the Union to be dissolved — I do not expect the house to fall — but I do expect it will cease to be divided"

107. D: The Underground Railroad didn't refer to an actual railroad or subway. It was a system of people, safe houses, and routes that were used to help southern slaves escape north to freedom. There were also "conductors" who would help lead bands of slaves. One of the most famous "conductors" was an escaped slave, Harriet Tubman the author of "Uncle Tom's Cabin".

108. B: With the Union's Conscription Act, a draftee could hire an "acceptable substitute" by paying $300 dollars, whereas in the Confederacy's Twenty Negro Law, anyone with at least 20 slaves could be exempted.

109. B: Senators from inland states that were considered part of the frontier in the 19th century were often concerned with transporting their crops and products to coastal areas in order to have access to markets and shipping. Henry Clay was from Kentucky, and therefore would represent Western interests. More infrastructure improvements (like canals, better roads, and eventually railroads) would benefit the West, as it would allow greater access for farmers to the markets of the Atlantic Seaboard. Often different regions of the country tended to see things only in relation to their interests. The North favored manufacturing and high, protective tariffs. The South was in favor of fugitive slave laws, low tariffs, and free trade. The West was agrarian, and part of the Frontier. They supported the relocation of Native American tribes in order to free up more land and also to decrease the threat of attacks from Native Americans. They also had less money for state sponsored improvements and therefore favored Federal funding for improvements.

110. D: Robert Owen purchased New Harmony, Indiana in order to establish a utopian community. He was a staunch critic of organized religion. New Harmony was based on communal utopian ideals, practiced collective ownership, and believed strongly in equality of all. All decisions were made as a group. They established an 8 hour work day. Because the community was based upon the

needs of its members, it is a reasonable inference that the founder of the town would have supported worker's rights.

111. D: The belief that people were free to choose God and salvation empowered them. Believing that they could change things through their actions and choices motivated people to pursue solutions to the many problems of the 19th century. Belief in free will helped people feel like their decisions and actions made a difference. This combined with a deep religious benevolence combined to produce strong actions to address the many and varied problems of society.

112. D: The election of 1844 was strongly divided along sectional lines. The North did not want to annex Texas as it would come in to the union as a slave state. However, they did want to acquire all of Oregon as part of manifest destiny. The South and West were staunchly pro-annexation (but for different reasons). Slavery, its continuation or abolition were very strong issues at this time. The Liberty Party was significant in the election as it took votes from Clay keeping him from winning New York which deprived him of the electoral votes and gave them to Polk. Religious liberty was not a strong issue in the country at the time.

113. B: Officially Andrew Johnson was impeached (i.e. accused) and brought to trial (in the Senate) over the firing of Secretary of War Edwin Stanton without the approval of Congress in violation of the Tenure of Office Act. Politically, however, the reasons for his impeachment were not so simple. Thaddeus Stevens and other radical Republicans disliked Johnson for his lenient Reconstruction plan and plotted to pass their own plan after his removal from office. The Senate acquitted Johnson by only one vote and he remained President. Many moderate Republicans joined with Democrats and would not allow the removal of a president for political reasons.

114. C: The War of 1812 is sometimes referred to as the 'War with no Outcome' because the Treaty of Ghent merely returned the borders to their pre-war limit. It failed to address the main issues that led to the war in the first place. It said nothing regarding British impressment of American sailors, nor did it guarantee the freedom of neutral American trading vessels. Hostilities ceased but no additions or losses of territory occurred.

115. B: The Monroe Doctrine, which was announced during Monroe's annual State of the Union Address, warned the European Powers that the United States would not allow further European colonization of the Western Hemisphere. The Monroe Doctrine was one of the defining points in the growth of the U.S. as a world power.

116. A: The Tariff of 1828 (also known as the Tariff of Abominations) was a protectionist tariff designed to shield northern industry from competition with imported European goods. The tariff was supported by many middle and New England states but opposed by the southern states which depended on cheaper European imports to supply the things they didn't manufacture. Due to the tariff, they were forced to buy more expensive Northern products. South Carolina refused to collect the tariff. Their legislature nullified the law saying it was unconstitutional and could not bind them. It was part of the growing sectional crisis that would culminate in the civil war. Henry Clay and John C. Calhoun proposed and helped pass a more acceptable tariff in 1833 to end the nullification crisis.

117. A: At many points in human history transitions of power between opposing political ideologies often resulted in armed resistance, revolution, and violence. What made the revolution of 1800 so "revolutionary" was that there was a peaceful transfer of power between strongly opposed political parties with very different views of what was best for the country. The fact that there was no armed insurrection made it stand out and is one of the great things about America. America has continued to transfer power between very different political groups every 4 years without armed unrest.

118. A: In *Marbury v. Madison*, John Marshall asserted the power of judicial review for the Supreme Court. The court could rule laws passed by Congress as unconstitutional. This was not stated anywhere in the Constitution. The Supreme Court gave itself its most significant power that was never stated or expressed in the constitution.

119. A: The Seneca Falls Convention of 1848 was organized by Elizabeth Cady Stanton and Lucretia Mott to discuss "the social, civil, and religious condition and rights of woman." Though women's rights advocates were often allied with abolitionists in the years leading up the Civil War the Seneca Falls convention was exclusively concerned with women's rights. In fact, abolitionist Frederick Douglass was the convention's only African American attendee and argued for the inclusion of a resolution in favor of women's suffrage to be debated during the meeting.

120. C: The Kansas Nebraska Act (1854) allowed popular sovereignty for the Kansas and Nebraska territories. Citizens of the two new territories would be able to vote whether they would become free or slave states upon applying to enter the union. The Kansas Nebraska Act was the final compromise attempt by Congress to address the issue of slavery before the start of the Civil War. Many were angered as it repealed the Missouri Compromise by potentially allowing slavery above the demarcation line. Part of the Act involved getting the territory organized in order to create a transcontinental railroad that linked Chicago and the West Coast. Various compromises were offered to help bring this about. Popular sovereignty was the compromise that finally helped bring about the organization of the territory. However, it led to bitter violence in Kansas (known as Bleeding Kansas). After a brutal internal civil war, Kansas was admitted to the union in 1861. But it was a moot victory as most of the Southern states had already seceded from the union.

How to Overcome Test Anxiety

Just the thought of taking a test is enough to make most people a little nervous. A test is an important event that can have a long-term impact on your future, so it's important to take it seriously and it's natural to feel anxious about performing well. But just because anxiety is normal, that doesn't mean that it's helpful in test taking, or that you should simply accept it as part of your life. Anxiety can have a variety of effects. These effects can be mild, like making you feel slightly nervous, or severe, like blocking your ability to focus or remember even a simple detail.

If you experience test anxiety—whether severe or mild—it's important to know how to beat it. To discover this, first you need to understand what causes test anxiety.

Causes of Test Anxiety

While we often think of anxiety as an uncontrollable emotional state, it can actually be caused by simple, practical things. One of the most common causes of test anxiety is that a person does not feel adequately prepared for their test. This feeling can be the result of many different issues such as poor study habits or lack of organization, but the most common culprit is time management. Starting to study too late, failing to organize your study time to cover all of the material, or being distracted while you study will mean that you're not well prepared for the test. This may lead to cramming the night before, which will cause you to be physically and mentally exhausted for the test. Poor time management also contributes to feelings of stress, fear, and hopelessness as you realize you are not well prepared but don't know what to do about it.

Other times, test anxiety is not related to your preparation for the test but comes from unresolved fear. This may be a past failure on a test, or poor performance on tests in general. It may come from comparing yourself to others who seem to be performing better or from the stress of living up to expectations. Anxiety may be driven by fears of the future—how failure on this test would affect your educational and career goals. These fears are often completely irrational, but they can still negatively impact your test performance.

> **Review Video:** <u>3 Reasons You Have Test Anxiety</u>
> Visit mometrix.com/academy and enter code: 428468

Elements of Test Anxiety

As mentioned earlier, test anxiety is considered to be an emotional state, but it has physical and mental components as well. Sometimes you may not even realize that you are suffering from test anxiety until you notice the physical symptoms. These can include trembling hands, rapid heartbeat, sweating, nausea, and tense muscles. Extreme anxiety may lead to fainting or vomiting. Obviously, any of these symptoms can have a negative impact on testing. It is important to recognize them as soon as they begin to occur so that you can address the problem before it damages your performance.

> **Review Video:** 3 Ways to Tell You Have Test Anxiety
> Visit mometrix.com/academy and enter code: 927847

The mental components of test anxiety include trouble focusing and inability to remember learned information. During a test, your mind is on high alert, which can help you recall information and stay focused for an extended period of time. However, anxiety interferes with your mind's natural processes, causing you to blank out, even on the questions you know well. The strain of testing during anxiety makes it difficult to stay focused, especially on a test that may take several hours. Extreme anxiety can take a huge mental toll, making it difficult not only to recall test information but even to understand the test questions or pull your thoughts together.

> **Review Video:** How Test Anxiety Affects Memory
> Visit mometrix.com/academy and enter code: 609003

Effects of Test Anxiety

Test anxiety is like a disease—if left untreated, it will get progressively worse. Anxiety leads to poor performance, and this reinforces the feelings of fear and failure, which in turn lead to poor performances on subsequent tests. It can grow from a mild nervousness to a crippling condition. If allowed to progress, test anxiety can have a big impact on your schooling, and consequently on your future.

Test anxiety can spread to other parts of your life. Anxiety on tests can become anxiety in any stressful situation, and blanking on a test can turn into panicking in a job situation. But fortunately, you don't have to let anxiety rule your testing and determine your grades. There are a number of relatively simple steps you can take to move past anxiety and function normally on a test and in the rest of life.

> **Review Video:** How Test Anxiety Impacts Your Grades
> Visit mometrix.com/academy and enter code: 939819

Physical Steps for Beating Test Anxiety

While test anxiety is a serious problem, the good news is that it can be overcome. It doesn't have to control your ability to think and remember information. While it may take time, you can begin taking steps today to beat anxiety.

Just as your first hint that you may be struggling with anxiety comes from the physical symptoms, the first step to treating it is also physical. Rest is crucial for having a clear, strong mind. If you are tired, it is much easier to give in to anxiety. But if you establish good sleep habits, your body and mind will be ready to perform optimally, without the strain of exhaustion. Additionally, sleeping well helps you to retain information better, so you're more likely to recall the answers when you see the test questions.

Getting good sleep means more than going to bed on time. It's important to allow your brain time to relax. Take study breaks from time to time so it doesn't get overworked, and don't study right before bed. Take time to rest your mind before trying to rest your body, or you may find it difficult to fall asleep.

> **Review Video: The Importance of Sleep for Your Brain**
> Visit mometrix.com/academy and enter code: 319338

Along with sleep, other aspects of physical health are important in preparing for a test. Good nutrition is vital for good brain function. Sugary foods and drinks may give a burst of energy but this burst is followed by a crash, both physically and emotionally. Instead, fuel your body with protein and vitamin-rich foods.

Also, drink plenty of water. Dehydration can lead to headaches and exhaustion, especially if your brain is already under stress from the rigors of the test. Particularly if your test is a long one, drink water during the breaks. And if possible, take an energy-boosting snack to eat between sections.

> **Review Video: How Diet Can Affect your Mood**
> Visit mometrix.com/academy and enter code: 624317

Along with sleep and diet, a third important part of physical health is exercise. Maintaining a steady workout schedule is helpful, but even taking 5-minute study breaks to walk can help get your blood pumping faster and clear your head. Exercise also releases endorphins, which contribute to a positive feeling and can help combat test anxiety.

When you nurture your physical health, you are also contributing to your mental health. If your body is healthy, your mind is much more likely to be healthy as well. So take time to rest, nourish your body with healthy food and water, and get moving as much as possible. Taking these physical steps will make you stronger and more able to take the mental steps necessary to overcome test anxiety.

> **Review Video: How to Stay Healthy and Prevent Test Anxiety**
> Visit mometrix.com/academy and enter code: 877894

Mental Steps for Beating Test Anxiety

Working on the mental side of test anxiety can be more challenging, but as with the physical side, there are clear steps you can take to overcome it. As mentioned earlier, test anxiety often stems from lack of preparation, so the obvious solution is to prepare for the test. Effective studying may be the most important weapon you have for beating test anxiety, but you can and should employ several other mental tools to combat fear.

First, boost your confidence by reminding yourself of past success—tests or projects that you aced. If you're putting as much effort into preparing for this test as you did for those, there's no reason you should expect to fail here. Work hard to prepare; then trust your preparation.

Second, surround yourself with encouraging people. It can be helpful to find a study group, but be sure that the people you're around will encourage a positive attitude. If you spend time with others who are anxious or cynical, this will only contribute to your own anxiety. Look for others who are motivated to study hard from a desire to succeed, not from a fear of failure.

Third, reward yourself. A test is physically and mentally tiring, even without anxiety, and it can be helpful to have something to look forward to. Plan an activity following the test, regardless of the outcome, such as going to a movie or getting ice cream.

When you are taking the test, if you find yourself beginning to feel anxious, remind yourself that you know the material. Visualize successfully completing the test. Then take a few deep, relaxing breaths and return to it. Work through the questions carefully but with confidence, knowing that you are capable of succeeding.

Developing a healthy mental approach to test taking will also aid in other areas of life. Test anxiety affects more than just the actual test—it can be damaging to your mental health and even contribute to depression. It's important to beat test anxiety before it becomes a problem for more than testing.

> **Review Video: Test Anxiety and Depression**
> Visit mometrix.com/academy and enter code: 904704

Study Strategy

Being prepared for the test is necessary to combat anxiety, but what does being prepared look like? You may study for hours on end and still not feel prepared. What you need is a strategy for test prep. The next few pages outline our recommended steps to help you plan out and conquer the challenge of preparation.

Step 1: Scope Out the Test

Learn everything you can about the format (multiple choice, essay, etc.) and what will be on the test. Gather any study materials, course outlines, or sample exams that may be available. Not only will this help you to prepare, but knowing what to expect can help to alleviate test anxiety.

Step 2: Map Out the Material

Look through the textbook or study guide and make note of how many chapters or sections it has. Then divide these over the time you have. For example, if a book has 15 chapters and you have five days to study, you need to cover three chapters each day. Even better, if you have the time, leave an extra day at the end for overall review after you have gone through the material in depth.

If time is limited, you may need to prioritize the material. Look through it and make note of which sections you think you already have a good grasp on, and which need review. While you are studying, skim quickly through the familiar sections and take more time on the challenging parts. Write out your plan so you don't get lost as you go. Having a written plan also helps you feel more in control of the study, so anxiety is less likely to arise from feeling overwhelmed at the amount to cover. A sample plan may look like this:

- Day 1: Skim chapters 1–4, study chapter 5 (especially pages 31–33)
- Day 2: Study chapters 6–7, skim chapters 8–9
- Day 3: Skim chapter 10, study chapters 11–12 (especially pages 87–90)
- Day 4: Study chapters 13–15
- Day 5: Overall review (focus most on chapters 5, 6, and 12), take practice test

Step 3: Gather Your Tools

Decide what study method works best for you. Do you prefer to highlight in the book as you study and then go back over the highlighted portions? Or do you type out notes of the important information? Or is it helpful to make flashcards that you can carry with you? Assemble the pens, index cards, highlighters, post-it notes, and any other materials you may need so you won't be distracted by getting up to find things while you study.

If you're having a hard time retaining the information or organizing your notes, experiment with different methods. For example, try color-coding by subject with colored pens, highlighters, or post-it notes. If you learn better by hearing, try recording yourself reading your notes so you can listen while in the car, working out, or simply sitting at your desk. Ask a friend to quiz you from your flashcards, or try teaching someone the material to solidify it in your mind.

Step 4: Create Your Environment

It's important to avoid distractions while you study. This includes both the obvious distractions like visitors and the subtle distractions like an uncomfortable chair (or a too-comfortable couch that makes you want to fall asleep). Set up the best study environment possible: good lighting and a comfortable work area. If background music helps you focus, you may want to turn it on, but otherwise keep the room quiet. If you are using a computer to take notes, be sure you don't have any other windows open, especially applications like social media, games, or anything else that could distract you. Silence your phone and turn off notifications. Be sure to keep water close by so you stay hydrated while you study (but avoid unhealthy drinks and snacks).

Also, take into account the best time of day to study. Are you freshest first thing in the morning? Try to set aside some time then to work through the material. Is your mind clearer in the afternoon or evening? Schedule your study session then. Another method is to study at the same time of day that you will take the test, so that your brain gets used to working on the material at that time and will be ready to focus at test time.

Step 5: Study!

Once you have done all the study preparation, it's time to settle into the actual studying. Sit down, take a few moments to settle your mind so you can focus, and begin to follow your study plan. Don't give in to distractions or let yourself procrastinate. This is your time to prepare so you'll be ready to fearlessly approach the test. Make the most of the time and stay focused.

Of course, you don't want to burn out. If you study too long you may find that you're not retaining the information very well. Take regular study breaks. For example, taking five minutes out of every hour to walk briskly, breathing deeply and swinging your arms, can help your mind stay fresh.

As you get to the end of each chapter or section, it's a good idea to do a quick review. Remind yourself of what you learned and work on any difficult parts. When you feel that you've mastered the material, move on to the next part. At the end of your study session, briefly skim through your notes again.

But while review is helpful, cramming last minute is NOT. If at all possible, work ahead so that you won't need to fit all your study into the last day. Cramming overloads your brain with more information than it can process and retain, and your tired mind may struggle to recall even previously learned information when it is overwhelmed with last-minute study. Also, the urgent nature of cramming and the stress placed on your brain contribute to anxiety. You'll be more likely to go to the test feeling unprepared and having trouble thinking clearly.

So don't cram, and don't stay up late before the test, even just to review your notes at a leisurely pace. Your brain needs rest more than it needs to go over the information again. In fact, plan to finish your studies by noon or early afternoon the day before the test. Give your brain the rest of the day to relax or focus on other things, and get a good night's sleep. Then you will be fresh for the test and better able to recall what you've studied.

Step 6: Take a practice test

Many courses offer sample tests, either online or in the study materials. This is an excellent resource to check whether you have mastered the material, as well as to prepare for the test format and environment.

Check the test format ahead of time: the number of questions, the type (multiple choice, free response, etc.), and the time limit. Then create a plan for working through them. For example, if you have 30 minutes to take a 60-question test, your limit is 30 seconds per question. Spend less time on the questions you know well so that you can take more time on the difficult ones.

If you have time to take several practice tests, take the first one open book, with no time limit. Work through the questions at your own pace and make sure you fully understand them. Gradually work up to taking a test under test conditions: sit at a desk with all study materials put away and set a timer. Pace yourself to make sure you finish the test with time to spare and go back to check your answers if you have time.

After each test, check your answers. On the questions you missed, be sure you understand why you missed them. Did you misread the question (tests can use tricky wording)? Did you forget the information? Or was it something you hadn't learned? Go back and study any shaky areas that the practice tests reveal.

Taking these tests not only helps with your grade, but also aids in combating test anxiety. If you're already used to the test conditions, you're less likely to worry about it, and working through tests until you're scoring well gives you a confidence boost. Go through the practice tests until you feel comfortable, and then you can go into the test knowing that you're ready for it.

Test Tips

On test day, you should be confident, knowing that you've prepared well and are ready to answer the questions. But aside from preparation, there are several test day strategies you can employ to maximize your performance.

First, as stated before, get a good night's sleep the night before the test (and for several nights before that, if possible). Go into the test with a fresh, alert mind rather than staying up late to study.

Try not to change too much about your normal routine on the day of the test. It's important to eat a nutritious breakfast, but if you normally don't eat breakfast at all, consider eating just a protein bar. If you're a coffee drinker, go ahead and have your normal coffee. Just make sure you time it so that the caffeine doesn't wear off right in the middle of your test. Avoid sugary beverages, and drink enough water to stay hydrated but not so much that you need a restroom break 10 minutes into the test. If your test isn't first thing in the morning, consider going for a walk or doing a light workout before the test to get your blood flowing.

Allow yourself enough time to get ready, and leave for the test with plenty of time to spare so you won't have the anxiety of scrambling to arrive in time. Another reason to be early is to select a good seat. It's helpful to sit away from doors and windows, which can be distracting. Find a good seat, get out your supplies, and settle your mind before the test begins.

When the test begins, start by going over the instructions carefully, even if you already know what to expect. Make sure you avoid any careless mistakes by following the directions.

Then begin working through the questions, pacing yourself as you've practiced. If you're not sure on an answer, don't spend too much time on it, and don't let it shake your confidence. Either skip it and come back later, or eliminate as many wrong answers as possible and guess among the remaining ones. Don't dwell on these questions as you continue—put them out of your mind and focus on what lies ahead.

Be sure to read all of the answer choices, even if you're sure the first one is the right answer. Sometimes you'll find a better one if you keep reading. But don't second-guess yourself if you do immediately know the answer. Your gut instinct is usually right. Don't let test anxiety rob you of the information you know.

If you have time at the end of the test (and if the test format allows), go back and review your answers. Be cautious about changing any, since your first instinct tends to be correct, but make sure you didn't misread any of the questions or accidentally mark the wrong answer choice. Look over any you skipped and make an educated guess.

At the end, leave the test feeling confident. You've done your best, so don't waste time worrying about your performance or wishing you could change anything. Instead, celebrate the successful completion of this test. And finally, use this test to learn how to deal with anxiety even better next time.

> **Review Video: 5 Tips to Beat Test Anxiety**
> Visit mometrix.com/academy and enter code: 570656

Important Qualification

Not all anxiety is created equal. If your test anxiety is causing major issues in your life beyond the classroom or testing center, or if you are experiencing troubling physical symptoms related to your anxiety, it may be a sign of a serious physiological or psychological condition. If this sounds like your situation, we strongly encourage you to seek professional help.

Thank You

We at Mometrix would like to extend our heartfelt thanks to you, our friend and patron, for allowing us to play a part in your journey. It is a privilege to serve people from all walks of life who are unified in their commitment to building the best future they can for themselves.

The preparation you devote to these important testing milestones may be the most valuable educational opportunity you have for making a real difference in your life. We encourage you to put your heart into it—that feeling of succeeding, overcoming, and yes, conquering will be well worth the hours you've invested.

We want to hear your story, your struggles and your successes, and if you see any opportunities for us to improve our materials so we can help others even more effectively in the future, please share that with us as well. **The team at Mometrix would be absolutely thrilled to hear from you!** So please, send us an email (support@mometrix.com) and let's stay in touch.

If you'd like some additional help, check out these other resources we offer for your exam:

http://MometrixFlashcards.com/CLEP

Additional Bonus Material

Due to our efforts to try to keep this book to a manageable length, we've created a link that will give you access to all of your additional bonus material.

Please visit http://www.mometrix.com/bonus948/clepushisti to access the information.